MIND-BLOWING FACTS FOR THE EVER-CURIOUS

FASCINATING, WEIRD, AND WONDERFUL TRUTHS TO AMAZE YOUR FRIENDS, CHALLENGE YOUR THINKING, AND KEEP YOU ENTERTAINED FOR HOURS

GLORIA LEMBO

© **Copyright Gloria Lembo 2025 - All rights reserved.**

Legal Notice:

This book is copyright protected. This book is only for personal use. The content within this book may not be reproduced, duplicated or transmitted without direct written permission from the author or the publisher.

You cannot amend, distribute, sell, use, quote or paraphrase any part, of the content within this book, without the consent of the author or publisher.

Disclaimer Notice:

Please note the information contained within this document is for educational and entertainment purposes only. All effort has been expended to present accurate, up-to-date, and reliable, complete information. No warranties of any kind are declared or implied. Readers acknowledge that the author is not engaging in the rendering of legal, financial, medical, or professional advice. The content within this book has been derived from various sources. Please consult a licensed professional before attempting any techniques outlined in this book. You are responsible for your own choices, actions, and results.

By reading this document, the reader agrees that under no circumstances is the author responsible for any losses, direct or indirect, which are incurred as a result of the use of the information contained within this document, including, but not limited to errors, omissions, or inaccuracies. Under no circumstances will any blame or legal responsibility be held against the publisher, or author, for any damages, reparation, or monetary loss due to the information contained within this book, either directly or indirectly.

Dedicated to Byron

May you always stay "Ever-Curious"

CONTENTS

Introduction	9
1. UNBELIEVABLE ANIMAL KINGDOM	13
The Immortal Jellyfish: A Creature That Defies Aging	14
The Mimic Octopus: Nature's Ultimate Impersonator	16
Shrimp with a Sonic Boom: The Mantis Shrimp	19
The Giraffe: Nature's Elegant Oddball	22
Elephants: Big Feet, Bigger Feelings	25
Ants: Masters of Miniature Civilizations	28
Dreaming with One Eye Open: How Dolphins Sleep	31
The Surprising Navigation Skills of Pigeons	33
Whale Songs: Ballards Beneath the Waves	36
2. SCIENCE & NATURAL WONDERS	39
The Wood Wide Web: The Secret Network of Trees	40
The Secret Lives of Fungi: Nature's Recyclers	42
The Weight of Clouds: A Million Pounds of Floating Water	45
Nature's Desert Symphony: Singing Sand Dunes	47
The Magic of Bioluminescent Waters	50
Frozen and Spinning: The Ice Discs That Dance in Rivers	53
The Scale of the Universe: Beyond Imagination	56
The Fermi Paradox: Where Is Everybody?	59
Quantum Entanglement: The Weirdest Love Story in Physics	63

3. MIND-BLOWING FACTS ABOUT HUMANS   67
   The Mystery of Phantom Limbs: When the
   Brain Plays Ghost   68
   Superhuman Strength: Adrenaline and Your
   Inner Superpower   71
   The Science of Synesthesia: Seeing Sounds and
   Tasting Colors   73
   The Incredible Regenerative Powers of the
   Human Liver   77
   The Astonishing Abilities of Supertasters 80
   The Science Behind Goosebumps, Yawning,
   and Other Body Quirks   82
   The Mysteries of Sleep Paralysis   85
   The Limits of Endurance: Human Body
   Extremes   88
   Epic Journeys Undertaken by Individuals 92

4. HISTORICAL ODDITIES   97
   The Dancing Plague of 1518   97
   The Mystery of the Voynich Manuscript 100
   The London Beer Flood: The Day Ale Took
   Over the Streets   103
   The Lost City of Z: Elusive Legends of
   Exploration   106
   The Disappearance of the Roanoke Colony 110
   The Year Without a Summer: 1816   113
   The Great Emu War: Australia's Flightless Foes 116
   The Man Who Survived Two Atomic Bombs 119
   The Cadaver Synod: When a Pope Put a Dead
   Pope on Trial   122

5. EVERYDAY THINGS YOU DIDN'T KNOW
   HAD A SECRET HISTORY   127
   Going in Style: The Strange, Civilizing History
   of Toilets and TP   128
   X-Rays: The Invisible Discovery That Changed
   Medicine   131
   Microwave Ovens: A Melted Candy Bar
   Changed the Kitchen   134
   Penicillin: The Moldy Mistake That Saves
   Millions   137

The Sticky Inspiration from Nature	140
The Post-It Note: An Accidental Invention	142
Crispy Revenge: The Origin of the Potato Chip	145
The Unexpected Origins of the Toothbrush	147
Corn Flakes: Breakfast's Most Accidental Icon	151
6. BIZARRE COINCIDENCES & SYNCHRONICITIES	155
The Twin Brothers with Identical Lives	156
The Eerie Coincidences of the Titanic and the Titan	159
Lincoln and Kennedy: Parallels Beyond Belief	162
Sir Anthony Hopkins: When the Universe Casts the Right Actor	165
History's Perfect Timing: The Day Jefferson and Adams Died	168
A Dam Strange Coincidence: The Tierneys and the Hoover Dam	171
Eerie Patterns Behind a National Tragedy	174
Carl Jung's Meaningful Coincidences	177
Conclusion	181
References	185

INTRODUCTION

Did you know that a shrimp can snap its claw so fast it creates a sonic boom or that a single cloud can weigh over a million pounds? These are real, mind-blowing facts about the world we live in. And they're just the beginning.

If you're the kind of person who lights up when you learn something new, surprising, or just plain weird, this book is for you.

This collection is my tribute to curiosity. I've gathered some of the most astonishing, conversation-starting facts across a wide range of topics. Each one was chosen to delight, intrigue, and maybe even make you say, "*Wait... what?!*" Facts that seem too bizarre to be true but absolutely are. I've done my homework, digging through the details, fact-checking every oddity. I made sure each tidbit is as accurate as it is entertaining.

Unlike many fact books that provide hundreds of one-liners or short blurbs, I've chosen to take a different route. It's one that I believe makes the experience more memorable. Every fact in this book is wrapped in a short story. A narrative. A little journey. Because stories don't just entertain us; they help us remember. When you connect a fact to a surprising event, a quirky personality, or an unforgettable twist, it sticks with you. That's what makes these pages different. They don't just inform. They invite you in.

And for the extra curious, I added a *"To Learn More"* section at the end of each story. If you want to dive deeper or explore the science behind the strange, you'll find links to hand-picked articles, videos, and book recommendations that expand on the topic. To make visiting them easier, I've converted their web addresses into simple, user-friendly TinyURLs.

Here's a taste of what's inside:

- **Unbelievable Animal Kingdom** – Meet the oddball giraffe, the immortal jellyfish, and the shape-shifting mimic octopus.
- **Science & Nature Wonders** – Discover hidden tree networks, spinning ice circles, and the weirdest love story in physics.
- **Mind-Blowing Facts About Humans** – Explore the mysteries of phantom limbs, the quirks of our biology, and real-life feats of superhuman strength.
- **Historical Oddities** – From dancing plagues to the year without a summer, history is filled with events so bizarre, you'd think they were made up. But somehow, it's all true.
- **Everyday Things You Didn't Know Had a Secret History** – Your toilet, toothbrush, microwave, Post-

it Notes, and even Corn Flakes have backstories that are anything but ordinary.
- **Bizarre Coincidences & Synchronicities** – The universe seems to have a sense of humor. These eerie parallels and jaw-dropping coincidences may make you wonder if everything is truly connected.

You won't find dry textbook stuff here: just curious, quirky, and easy-to-read stories designed to make you smile and say, *"Wow, I had no idea!"*

Whether you're 9 or 99, this book is your pass to the weird, the wild, and the wonderfully true. You're about to go on a fact-filled adventure that's anything but ordinary.

1

UNBELIEVABLE ANIMAL KINGDOM

Welcome to the wild side of wonder, where jellyfish can cheat death, octopuses pull off underwater impersonations, and dolphins quite literally sleep with one eye open. In this chapter, animals take center stage. Animals aren't just fascinating; they're downright unbelievable. From whales that compose deep-sea ballads to the elegant oddball giraffe, these creatures challenge what we thought we knew about instinct, intelligence, and survival. Get ready to meet nature's greatest show-offs that will have you laughing, gasping, and marveling at just how clever, weird, and truly wild Mother Nature can be.

THE IMMORTAL JELLYFISH: A CREATURE THAT DEFIES AGING

What if you could grow old and then start over again? No creams, no time machines, just a complete biological reboot. That's exactly what a tiny sea creature called *Turritopsis dohrnii* can do. Often nicknamed the "immortal jellyfish," this unassuming little marvel has one of the most jaw-dropping abilities in the animal kingdom. It can reverse its aging process and return to its youthful state whenever life gets rough.

Stress, injury, starvation? For most creatures, that's game over. But not this jellyfish. It pulls off the ultimate vanishing act by transforming itself back into a baby version of itself, starting its life cycle anew. This miraculous process is called transdifferentiation, a cellular trick where one type of cell transforms into another. It's like your skin cells suddenly deciding to become brain cells and pulling it off without a hitch.

Initially discovered in the Mediterranean, *Turritopsis dohrnii* is no bigger than a pinky nail. But its secret to longevity has caused a stir among scientists. Once it hits adulthood and things go south, it doesn't just ride it out. It hits the reset button and morphs back into a polyp, its earliest stage of life. Then, like a biological Groundhog Day, it can grow up all over again. *And again. And again.*

Of course, "immortal" doesn't mean invincible. The jellyfish can still fall prey to predators, disease, or environmental changes. But if left undisturbed? It may never die of old age.

Researchers are fascinated by how this humble jellyfish could hold clues to human aging, cancer resistance, and regenerative medicine. Its DNA has now been sequenced, revealing genes linked to cell repair and longevity. It's as if nature has handed us a microscopic cheat sheet on how to outsmart aging itself.

So, while it might not look like much, just a transparent blob pulsing through the sea, *Turritopsis dohrnii* might be one of the most incredible survivors on the planet. Proof that in the game of life, sometimes the smallest players have the biggest tricks up their (gelatinous) sleeves.

Fascinating Facts

- Size doesn't matter: Despite its mind-blowing ability, the immortal jellyfish is tiny—only about the size of a pinky fingernail.
- Not truly invincible: While it can theoretically live forever, it's still vulnerable to predators, disease, and environmental threats.
- Biomedical Interest: Scientists are studying *Turritopsis dohrnii* for potential clues to unlocking anti-aging mechanisms in humans.

To Learn More

- Orozco, Trizzy. "Why the Immortal Jellyfish May Never Die and What That Means for Aging." *Discover*

Wild Science, May 6, 2025. This article explores the biology of the immortal jellyfish and how its unique life cycle could reshape our understanding of aging and longevity. https://tinyurl.com/jellyfish-immortal
- Osterloff, Emily. "Immortal jellyfish: the secret to cheating death." *Natural History Museum*. Discover how Turritopsis dohrnii, the so-called "immortal jellyfish," reverses its life cycle to potentially live forever. This site includes a very good National History Museum video. https://tinyurl.com/immortal-jellyfish-secret
- Real Science. "The Incredible Way This Jellyfish Goes Back in Time". *YouTube*, May 21, 2022. This video explains the mind-blowing process that lets a jellyfish essentially rewind its biological clock—again and again. https://tinyurl.com/immortal-jellyfish-video

THE MIMIC OCTOPUS: NATURE'S ULTIMATE IMPERSONATOR

You're snorkeling in warm, murky waters, and you spot what appears to be a venomous sea snake. You blink, and suddenly, it's a lionfish with its spiny fins fanned out. Blink again, and now it's a flatfish gliding along the seafloor. But it's none of these. You've just encountered the master of disguise. Meet the mimic octopus (*Thaumoctopus mimicus*), nature's ultimate shapeshifter and one of the ocean's most astonishing examples of intelligence and deception.

Discovered in 1998 near Sulawesi, Indonesia, the mimic octopus is a relatively recent addition to the catalog of marine marvels. This ingenious invertebrate takes deception to theatrical levels, impersonating over 15 different marine species (including lionfish, sea snakes, flatfish, and jellyfish) to outwit predators and prey alike.

How does it pull off these quick-change acts? The mimic octopus utilizes specialized skin cells called chromatophores. These chromatophores enable it to rapidly change its color and pattern. It's like having a costume party underwater.

But it doesn't stop there. By contorting its body and limbs, it can mimic the shape and movements of other sea creatures. For instance, to imitate a lionfish, it spreads its arms wide and undulates them to resemble the fish's spines. To mimic a sea snake, it hides six arms. It waves the remaining two in opposite directions, creating the illusion of a slithering serpent.

This mimicry isn't just a flashy party trick. It's a sophisticated survival strategy. The mimic octopus lives in open, muddy, and perilous waters, where hiding spots are few and predators are plenty. So instead of running (which is hard with no legs) or hiding (which is tough with no cover), it opts for the next best thing: *becoming something scarier.*

When danger looms, this eight-armed illusionist scans the scene and makes a split-second decision. Should it channel its inner venomous sea snake, spooky flatfish, or prickly lionfish today? Observations suggest it actually chooses its costume based on which predator is lurking nearby.

This isn't just mimicry; it's nature's version of performance art. The mimic octopus is both actor and director, crafting a convincing act complete with movement, flair, and character motivation. It doesn't just imitate, it embodies.

It's a dazzling reminder that sometimes, in nature's theater, the smartest defense isn't brute force or speed. It's about putting on the right costume and playing your part as if your life depended on it. Because in the mimic octopus's world, it often does.

Fascinating Facts

- Master of Disguise: The mimic octopus can impersonate at least 15 different marine species, including lionfish, flatfish, and sea snakes. Found in muddy, open environments with few hiding places, its survival depends on the creativity of its camouflage.
- Smart Shapeshifter: It not only mimics appearance, but also adjusts behavior and movement to match the species it's imitating. They are natural problem-solvers.
- Neural Network: Octopuses are highly intelligent. They have approximately 500 million neurons, more than some mammals, and most of these neurons are located in their arms.

To Learn More

- American Museum of Natural History. "The Talented Mimic Octopus." *AMNH News & Blogs*, June 23, 2015. Learn how the mimic octopus strategically imitates toxic animals like lionfish and sea snakes to survive in the wild. https://tinyurl.com/talented-mimic-octopus
- Getty Images TV. "Mimic Octopus: Master of Disguise." *YouTube*, October 11, 2017. This video showcases the mimic octopus in action, highlighting its incredible ability to morph into multiple marine species in real time. https://tinyurl.com/mimic-octopus-video
- Spencer, Erin. "Why the Mimic Octopus is the Ultimate Master of Disguise." *Ocean Conservancy*, April 2022. This blog describes the mimic octopus's unparalleled camouflage skills and why it's considered nature's ultimate impersonator. This site also includes a very good video. https://tinyurl.com/mimic-octopus-disguise-master

SHRIMP WITH A SONIC BOOM: THE MANTIS SHRIMP

Meet the mantis shrimp: a small, vibrant marine crustacean that packs a powerful punch. This punchy little powerhouse doesn't just throw a jab. It unleashes a strike so fast it boils water, creates a flash of light, and unleashes a shockwave strong enough to shatter glass. All that from a creature no bigger than a hot dog.

There are two kinds of mantis shrimp: *spearers*, who skewer prey with needle-like precision, and *smashers*, who bring the pain with club-like appendages that move at 50 miles per hour (80 kph). That's so fast it creates something called cavitation bubbles (pockets of low-pressure vapor.) These bubbles collapse with such force they generate heat, light, and sound, essentially creating a tiny underwater shockwave or "sonic boom." Translation? This means the mantis shrimp hits its target twice: once with its claw and again with the collapsing bubble. That's enough power to break aquarium glass and crack open tough-shelled prey like crabs and snails. Imagine knocking out your dinner with a punch before eating it!

Even its armor is next-level. Their striking appendage is built like a natural baseball bat, reinforced with a herringbone pattern. It is strong enough to absorb shock without shattering. Engineers are so impressed that they're studying it to inspire next-generation body armor and aircraft materials.

But the mantis shrimp isn't just a warrior. It's also got supervision. While humans perceive color through three channels (red, green, and blue), the mantis shrimp has up to 16 channels, including ones that detect ultraviolet and polarized light. It's like seeing in a secret language of color and sparkle we can't even comprehend.

In short, it's fast, it's fierce, it's fashionable (those colors!), and it can see the world in a way that would make Superman jealous. The mantis shrimp is living proof that sometimes the fiercest warriors come in the smallest packages.

Fascinating Facts

- Lightning Speed: The mantis shrimp has the world's fastest punch. Their punch has the same acceleration as a 22-calibre bullet.
- Super Vision: They can detect polarized light and see into the ultraviolet spectrum with compound eyes that move independently.
- Biomechanical Marvel: Their club-like appendages are so strong and shock-resistant that they're being studied for advanced materials engineering.

To Learn More

- Hashemi, Sara. "Mantis Shrimp Pact a Punch With the Force of a Bullet – and They Don't Get Hurt. Here's How." *Smithsonian Magazine Smart News*, February 13, 2025. This article reveals how mantis shrimp deliver blows as fast as a bullet without injuring themselves. https://tinyurl.com/mantis-shrimp-bullet-punch
- Nat Geo Animals. "Mantis Shrimp Packs a Punch, Predator in Paradise" *YouTube*, May 29, 2019. This excellent video showcases the mantic shrimp in action. https://tinyurl.com/mantis-shrimp-predator
- Nightingale, Sarah. "Mantis shrimp inspires next generation of ultra-strong materials." *University of California*, May 31, 2016. Learn how researchers are using the mantis shrimp's ultra-tough appendages as

a blueprint for developing next-gen materials that are lightweight yet incredibly impact-resistant.
https://tinyurl.com/mantis-shrimp-next-gen

THE GIRAFFE: NATURE'S ELEGANT ODDBALL

Giraffes look like they were designed during a brainstorming session that got out of hand: a bit of horse here, some leopard spots there, a dinosaur's neck, eyelashes of a runway model, and a hint of cartoon charm. But behind their lanky elegance lies one of nature's most spectacular success stories. They're tough, strategic, and surprisingly strange.

Let's start with the basics: giraffes are the tallest land animals on Earth. Adult males can reach up to 18 feet (5.5 meters) tall, and their necks alone stretch more than 6 feet (1.8 meters). But here's the twist: just like you and me, they have seven neck vertebrae. The difference is that theirs are just over 10 inches long. Stacked together, they form a towering structure that allows giraffes to snack on tree leaves that no other creature can reach.

When it comes to dining, giraffes don't mess around. They're leaf-stripping machines. A hungry adult can munch up to 75 pounds (34 kg) of foliage a day, most of it plucked from thorny trees like acacias. Luckily, they come equipped with 20-inch tongues that work like nature's salad tongs, nimble enough to strip leaves with precision. Their extra-thick saliva adds another layer of protection, keeping their mouths safe from sharp thorns. And here's a bonus quirk. Those long tongues are a striking blue-black color, a natural sunscreen that helps prevent sunburn during their all-day snacking sessions under the African sun.

Atop their heads sit ossicones, those horn-like protrusions that are actually bony structures covered in skin and fur. Unlike true horns, ossicones are present from birth. They serve various functions, from managing core body temperature to aiding in combat.

Despite their gentle look, giraffes are not to be underestimated. Their 12-inch hooves can kick hard enough to kill a lion. And they're no slouches in a sprint. Giraffes can run up to 35 miles per hour, leaving even most horses in the dust.

But giraffe combat isn't all kicks and chaos. Male giraffes also engage in a peculiar ritual called "necking." No, it's not romantic. It's a full-body, slow-motion duel where they swing their heads at each other to establish dominance. Sometimes, the battles look comically slow; other times, they get fierce enough to knock a rival off his hooves.

The next time you spot a giraffe stretching that towering neck for a leafy snack, take a moment to appreciate the marvel before you. Giraffes aren't just nature's gentle giants. They're one of its most bizarre, beautiful, and unforgettable masterpieces.

Fascinating Facts

- Julius Caesar brought the Giraffe to Rome: Julius Caesar introduced the first known giraffe to Europe in 46 BC. It was probably a gift from Cleopatria. After showing it off to the people of Rome, he ended up feeding it to the lions.
- Falling into Life: Giraffes give birth standing up, and the calf drops about six feet. That first tumble actually helps stimulate the calf to start breathing. Within 10 hours, that baby is up and running, ready to join the herd.
- Style: No two giraffes have the same pattern of spots. Each coat is as unique as a fingerprint.
- Silent Extinction: There are approximately 117,000 wild giraffes worldwide, a decline of nearly 30% since the 1980s. The population of northern giraffes has declined from 25,653 to 5,919, around a 77% decline.

To Learn More

- GCF. "Wonders of the giraffe's world." *Giraffe Conservation Foundation.* Provides comprehensive coverage of the science and conservation efforts behind the world's tallest land mammal, from its unique anatomy to the threats it faces in the wild. https://tinyurl.com/giraffe-wonders
- Robinson, Lizzie. "30 Most Random Facts About Giraffes." *The Fact Site*, April 1, 2025. This fun and quirky list rounds up some of the most surprising, weird, and delightful facts about giraffes you

probably didn't know. https://tinyurl.com/giraffes-facts
- Stuff to Blow Your Mind. "5 Amazing Giraffe Facts – Science on the Web #51" *YouTube,* April 20, 2014. This short video highlights five fascinating giraffe facts, blending science and wonder into one tall tale of nature's gentle giant. https://tinyurl.com/amazinggiraffe-video

ELEPHANTS: BIG FEET, BIGGER FEELINGS

If animals were handed out superpowers, elephants would be walking around with the complete set: strength, memory, empathy, and the uncanny ability to hear with their feet. *Yes, really.* These gentle giants aren't just enormous; they're emotionally complex, wildly perceptive, and equipped with some of the most remarkable built-in technology nature has to offer.

Let's start with the seismic stuff. Elephants can literally feel the Earth's heartbeat. Using special sensory cells in their padded feet and trunks, they can detect low-frequency rumbles known as infrasound. These are vibrations that travel through the ground and can come from miles away. It's how they pick up distant thunder, the approach of other herds, or even earthquakes before they arrive. Think of it as a built-in early warning system. Long before weather apps or text alerts, elephants were getting real-time updates on the world around them just by standing still.

But perhaps even more astonishing is their emotional intelligence. Elephants don't just remember; they feel deeply. When a member of their group dies, the rest of the herd doesn't just move on. They pause. They approach the body. They stroke it gently with their trunks. They stand in silence. And sometimes, they even return to the same spot years later. Scientists have observed elephants exhibiting behaviors so tender and human-like that it's hard not to be moved. These aren't random acts. They're rituals that speak to memory, grief, and maybe even love.

The secret to all this complexity? Brains. *Big ones.* Elephants have the largest brains of any land mammal, and they use them well. Their minds are wired for social connection, long-term memory, and empathy. They form lifelong friendships, recognize themselves in mirrors, and can remember water sources from years past. It's no wonder they're considered one of the most intelligent animals on Earth.

So yes, they're huge. But elephants aren't just the heavyweights of the savanna. They're also its emotional core. They remind us that real power doesn't always roar. Sometimes, it rumbles softly beneath your feet and never forgets.

Fascinating Facts

- Sensing the Earth: Elephants can detect seismic waves from over 10 miles away through their feet and trunks, even before a storm or quake arrives.

- Grief and Memory: Elephants often mourn their dead, gently caressing bones, lingering at gravesites, and showing signs of emotional distress.
- Big Brains, Big Feelings: The average elephant's brain weighs about 10 to 12 pounds which supports advanced memory, empathy, and cooperation.

To Learn More

- Kennerson, Elliott. "How Elephants Listen ... With Their Feet." *KQED Deep Look,* July 17, 2018. This article, which includes a fascinating video, explores how elephants use their feet to detect distant sounds and seismic signals. https://tinyurl.com/elephants-listen-with-feet
- Parker, Laura. "Rare Video Shows Elephants 'Mourning' Matriarch's Death." *National Geographic,* August 21, 2016. This rare and moving video captures elephants gathering around a fallen matriarch, offering compelling evidence of their grief and emotional depth. https://tinyurl.com/elephants-mourning-video
- Wikipedia. "Elephant cognition." This article explores the remarkable intelligence of elephants, covering their problem-solving skills, memory, self-awareness, empathy, and complex social behaviors. https://tinyurl.com/elephant-cognition

ANTS: MASTERS OF MINIATURE CIVILIZATIONS

Imagine a bustling city, not of people but of ants, each one going about its job with purpose and precision. These tiny creatures have been quietly running complex societies beneath our feet for over *100 million years*.

Step into an ant colony (figuratively, of course), and you'll find a buzzing metropolis with strict job titles, division of labor, and zero slackers. At the center of it all is the queen. She's not a jeweled monarch with a throne, but a nonstop egg-laying powerhouse responsible for the colony's future population. She doesn't rule with an iron fist. She rules with biology. The real action belongs to the workers, who are basically the colony's all-purpose workforce: engineers, nurses, foragers, janitors, and farmers rolled into one.

And farmers they are, especially the leafcutter ants. These industrious little horticulturalists haul chunks of leaves back to their nests, not to eat but to feed their underground fungus gardens. That's right. Ants discovered farming long before humans did.

Meanwhile, soldier ants form the defense department, armed with powerful jaws and sometimes even chemical weapons, to protect the colony. Some take things to explosive levels, literally. Take *Camponotus saundersi*, a species of ant found in Southeast Asia. When threatened, they blow themselves up in a kamikaze-style defense, rupturing their bodies to release sticky, toxic goo that traps and deters attackers. It's as dramatic as it is effective.

Then there are ants that form living bridges with their bodies, raid everything in sight, and never stay in one place too long. Their entire colony moves in sync, devouring anything in their path with terrifying precision. On the other hand, species like the Argentine ant form sprawling supercolonies that can span thousands of miles, cooperating peacefully across regions with no internal conflict. World peace, but for ants.

Despite their size, ants have a massive impact on the environment. They aerate the soil as they tunnel. They help plants reproduce by dispersing seeds. They keep pest populations in check. They're the maintenance crew of the natural world, quietly holding ecosystems together with tireless teamwork.

So, how do they all coordinate without meetings, emails, or awkward Zoom calls? *Pheromones.* These are chemical messages ants release and follow like invisible text threads. One ant finds food and lays down a trail; the next one picks it up, reinforces it, and the line forms like ants at a Black Friday sale. Need a warning signal? There's a scent for that. Want to rally the troops? Just spray the alarm pheromone and watch the soldiers mobilize.

So, the next time you see a single ant scuttling across your picnic blanket, remember that little insect is part of a civilization. A civilization that rivals ours in complexity, strategy, and sheer determination. Who knew that under every rock was a miniature empire, humming along on instinct and a few chemical cues?

Fascinating Facts

- Job Specialization: Worker ants assume various roles, including foragers, builders, nurses, janitors, and more. Ants' jobs can change with age. As ants age, their jobs move them farther from the queen or the center of the colony.
- Scent-Based Communication: Ants use pheromones to share information, creating invisible maps for food, danger, and colony coordination.
- Colony Size: Ant colonies can range from a few dozen to millions. A supercolony occurs when many ant colonies over a large area unite.

To Learn More

- Ebs, Dylan. "25 Facts About Ants." *Oh My Facts,* October 25,2024. This fun fact list uncovers 25 surprising truths about ants. https://tinyurl.com/25-ant-facts
- Sammann, Stephanie. "The Insane Biology of Ant Colonies." *Real Science, YouTube.* February 6, 2021. This engaging video dives into the mind-blowing biology of ant colonies. https://tinyurl.com/ant-colonies-video
- Book recommendation: Campbell, Heather. "Ants: A Visual Guide." *Princeton University Press,* 2023. This beautifully illustrated guide showcases the astonishing diversity, structure, and behavior of ants, revealing their hidden complexity.

DREAMING WITH ONE EYE OPEN: HOW DOLPHINS SLEEP

If dolphins gave speeches, one of them might be titled: *"How to Sleep, Stay Alert, and Not Drown—All at Once."* Because that's precisely what they do.

Unlike us land-dwellers who blissfully drift into unconsciousness at night, dolphins have to be much more strategic about their snooze time. Why? Because dolphins are conscious breathers. They have to *think* about every breath they take. If they went fully offline as we do, they'd forget to come up for air, and, well … let's just say it wouldn't end well.

So, nature gave dolphins a brilliant backup plan: unihemispheric slow-wave sleep. That's a fancy way of saying they literally sleep with only half their brain at a time. One hemisphere powers down to rest, while the other stays on high alert, controlling breathing, watching for predators, and making sure they don't accidentally drift into shark territory.

And the eye opposite the sleeping brain? Closed. The other? Wide open and watching. It's like being the security guard and the napper at the same time. You'll often see them lazily swimming in circles or floating near the surface, one eye shut, just catching a little me-time without ever fully clocking out.

This split-brain snoozing isn't just a weird party trick; it's a survival superpower. It allows dolphins to rest while staying mobile and alert in a world where every shadow might spell danger. And with their incredibly social and intelligent nature, it makes perfect sense that dolphins evolved such a clever way to balance relaxation with awareness.

Scientists believe that this type of sleep also helps dolphins keep track of their pods. In fact, mothers and calves have been observed staying awake for days after birth, with the mother's brain remaining extra alert to protect her newborn. It's no wonder that dolphins are regarded as one of the ocean's most intelligent and socially complex creatures.

So next time you're having trouble falling asleep, just be glad you don't have to keep half your brain awake to remember to breathe on your own. Dolphins, it seems, are nature's original multitaskers.

Fascinating Facts

- Half-Brain Rest: Dolphins let one hemisphere sleep at a time, switching sides every few hours to stay alert and breathe.
- Conscious Breathing: They must actively surface for air, unlike humans who breathe automatically, even when asleep.
- One eye Open: The opposite eye stays open during sleep to help them watch for predators and maintain group awareness.

UNBELIEVABLE ANIMAL KINGDOM | 33

To Learn More

- Fagaly, Steve. "Do Dolphins Really Sleep with One Eye Open?" *Dolphins and You*, May 22, 2025. Find out how dolphins sleep while staying semi-alert to predators and surfacing for air—thanks to their incredible split-brain sleep strategy. https://tinyurl.com/dolphins-oneeye-sleeper
- Wild Matters. "How Do Dolphins Sleep?" *YouTube*, May 10, 2021. This video does a very good job of showing how dolphins manage to sleep without drowning. https://tinyurl.com/how-dolphins-sleep-video

THE SURPRISING NAVIGATION SKILLS OF PIGEONS

Pigeons might seem like ordinary city dwellers, but beneath those bobbing heads and fluttering wings lies a navigation system that would make GPS flinch.

Pigeons possess a remarkable sixth sense called magnetoreception, allowing them to detect the Earth's magnetic field. For years, scientists believed this superpower came from tiny particles of magnetite in their beaks that acted like microscopic compasses. More recent research suggests those iron-rich cells may actually be immune cells.

But magnetite may still play a supporting role. The mystery continues to flap in the wind.

But pigeons don't rely on just one trick. They are multisensory navigators who use a suite of tools that rivals any high-tech system. On sunny days, they track the sun's position to adjust their heading. On cloudy ones, they *sniff* their way home. That's right. Pigeons have an incredible sense of smell. In fact, scientists have shown that they create what are called olfactory maps: mental blueprints based on the unique scents carried by the wind. Whether it's the earthy smell of pine forests or the signature scent of a city, pigeons recognize and use these aromas to guide their journey.

When combined with their ability to recognize visual landmarks (buildings, rivers, mountain ranges), these birds become expert aerial cartographers. In controlled experiments, pigeons released far from home have been known to chart a return course with astonishing accuracy, often navigating terrain they've never seen before. No GPS. No map. Just instinct, smell, sunlight, and memory.

This uncanny homing ability made pigeons wartime VIPs. During World War I and II, homing pigeons were deployed to deliver vital messages across enemy lines. Despite bullets, bombs, and brutal weather, many succeeded in saving lives in the process. One pigeon, *Cher Ami*, became a decorated war hero. In 1918, this pigeon flew 25 miles in under 30 minutes to deliver a message that saved 194 soldiers. For his bravery, he was awarded the Croix de Guerre by the French government. Yes, some pigeons actually have war medals.

If that isn't impressive enough, pigeons are also surprisingly intelligent. They can recognize their own reflections in mirrors and learn complex tasks. They even grasp abstract concepts, something once thought to be exclusive to humans and great apes. In studies, they've distinguished between different art styles and even identified letters of the alphabet. It turns out "bird brain" might be more of a compliment than an insult.

The next time you see a pigeon pecking around a sidewalk take a moment to appreciate what you're really looking at: a feathered genius with a built-in compass, a scent-based GPS, wartime credentials, and a memory worthy of a seasoned world traveler. Pigeons aren't just part of the scenery. They're one of nature's greatest navigators, hiding in plain sight.

Fascinating Facts

- Sun Compass & Landmarks: Their navigation is fine-tuned by the sun's position and recognizable visual landmarks—even in unfamiliar terrain.
- Magnetic Masters: Pigeons use Earth's magnetic field as a navigational reference, similar to an internal compass.
- Excellent Eyesight: Pigeons possess excellent eyesight, enabling them to recognize and remember landmarks along familiar routes.
- Scent-Based Mapping: They create olfactory maps, using smells to build mental representations of large geographic areas.

To Learn More

- Xiang, Annie. "How Pigeons Find Their Home? The Secrets Behind Their Incredible Homing Ability." *Birdfly Blog*, September 18, 2024. This article explains the mystery of how pigeons navigate vast distances home using Earth's magnetic field, sun positioning, and even scent cues. https://tinyurl.com/pigeons-navigation
- Sammann, Stephanie. "How Pigeons Always Find Their Way Home". *Real Science YouTube*, June 12, 2022. This well-done video explores the science behind pigeons' astonishing homing skills, revealing how their brains function like natural GPS systems. https://tinyurl.com/pigeons-navigation-video

WHALE SONGS: BALLARDS BENEATH THE WAVES

Beneath the ocean's surface, a haunting concert of deep, rhythmic, melodic songs plays on repeat. No instruments, no speakers, just the majestic voice of a whale. It's real, and it comes from humpback whales, the true divas of the deep. These massive marine mammals belt out complex, eerie, and mesmerizing tunes that travel for thousands of miles through the sea. Their voices are not just loud; they're epic.

Male humpbacks are the soloists of this underwater concert. Their songs aren't random hoots or grunts. They're long, structured compositions, complete with rhythm, repetition, and refrains. Each "set" can last up to 30 minutes, and they may perform it on repeat for hours. And here's where it gets really wild: all the males in a given region sing the same version of the song at the same time. It's like the entire population is synced to the same oceanic Spotify playlist. But every few months, the tune evolves: new riffs are introduced, and old motifs fade out. The whales pick up on these changes and adjust their singing accordingly. It's not just singing. It's cultural transmission, a kind of underwater musical meme spreading across oceans.

And it's not just beautiful, *it's loud*. Humpback whale songs can be heard up to 10,000 miles (16,000 kilometers) away under the right oceanic conditions, thanks to low-frequency sound waves that travel incredibly efficiently through water. This means a single serenade might ripple across entire ocean basins. Scientists have even suggested that whales may be among the few animals capable of communicating on a global scale.

Why do they sing? That's still partly a mystery. The leading theory is that it's all about the ladies. Males likely sing to attract mates. However, there are other ideas: perhaps it's about establishing territory, coordinating group behavior, or simply enjoying the joy of singing. Who are we to deny a whale a bit of creative expression? What scientists do know is that these songs are shared, learned, and passed along from generation to generation. This makes humpbacks one of the few non-human species with a musical culture.

The next time you think only humans make art, consider the whale. A whale that is drifting through the deep, singing his heart out, sending a song across the planet that no one taught him, but everyone in his world seems to know.

Fascinating Facts

- Melodic Memory: Humpback whale songs can last up to 30 minutes and are repeated in cycles for hours.
- Global Reach: Whale songs can travel across entire ocean basins using low-frequency sound and special underwater channels.
- Cultural Evolution: Whale songs evolve over time and spread from one population to another, similar to musical trends in human cultures.

To Learn More

- 3D Sailor. "Humpback whales sing beautifully." *YouTube,* August 31, 2022. This captivating video lets you experience the hauntingly beautiful songs of humpback whales echoing through the deep blue. https://tinyurl.com/humpback-video
- Briggs, Helen and Gill, Victoria. "Whale song mystery solved by scientists." *BBC News,* February 21, 2024. Scientists may have finally cracked the code behind humpback whale songs, revealing how these complex vocalizations help males broadcast their presence over vast distances. https://tinyurl.com/humpback-song-mystery-solved

2

SCIENCE & NATURAL WONDERS

Science has never looked so strange or so fascinating. In this chapter, you'll discover some of Earth's most jaw-dropping natural wonders, the kind that make you look twice and say, *"Wait, that's real?"* We're diving into forests that whisper through underground root networks like secret societies, oceans that glow like magical potions every time you splash them, and clouds so heavy they could crush a skyscraper yet float like feathers. From quantum particles that seem to break the rules of reality to cosmic marvels that make us feel wonderfully small, this is science with a serious sense of wonder.

THE WOOD WIDE WEB: THE SECRET NETWORK OF TREES

If you thought trees were solitary, silent giants, think again. Beneath the forest floor lies an underground network so intricate and efficient that it's been dubbed the "Wood Wide Web." This vast, living communication system, powered by fungi, enables trees to share resources, exchange messages, and even warn one another of danger. It's one of nature's most fascinating secrets.

At the center of this natural network are *mycorrhizal fungi*, microscopic powerhouses that connect tree roots through threadlike structures called hyphae. Through this living internet, trees share everything from food to danger alerts. It's not just survival. It's cooperation. Through these microscopic connections, trees can transfer water, nutrients, and chemical signals to one another. In other words, they're talking silently, invisibly, and constantly.

Older, established "Mother Trees" act like the wise elders of the forest, funneling nutrients to younger saplings and helping them get a strong start. Forests aren't a battlefield. They're a family!

Dr. Suzanne Simard, a pioneering forest ecologist from the University of British Columbia, transformed our understanding of how trees interact. Not only do they share nutrients, they also communicate danger to one another.

Her research demonstrated that forests are cooperative communities. And get this: when a tree is attacked by pests, it sends chemical warnings through the network. Neighboring trees receive the signal and start ramping up their own defenses, like producing bitter-tasting chemicals to keep the pests away. It's a botanical version of texting: *"Danger ahead, brace yourselves!"* Who knew trees had a neighborhood watch?

Fascinating Facts

- Mother Trees' Reach: A single mature tree can be connected to hundreds of other trees through underground fungal networks. Interestingly, hours before and during a solar eclipse, electrical activity between trees becomes significantly more synchronized. The mature trees have a more pronounced early response that guides the collective response of the whole forest.
- Fungal Partners: *Mycorrhizal fungi* are believed to connect up to 90% of all land plants, forming one of Earth's most widespread symbioses.
- Impact of Deforestation: Disrupting the Wood Wide Web can significantly slow forest recovery and increase vulnerability to pests and droughts.

To Learn More

- Grant, Richard. "Do Trees Talk to Each Other?" *Ask Smithsonian*, March 2018. This article explores groundbreaking research suggesting that trees communicate through underground fungal networks

—sharing resources, warnings, and wisdom across the forest floor. https://tinyurl.com/do-trees-talk
- Suzanne Simard's TED Talk: "How Trees Talk to Each Other." *TED*, June 2016. Ecologist Suzanne Simard reveals how trees form intricate social networks, nurturing seedlings and exchanging nutrients through a hidden web of roots and fungi. https://tinyurl.com/how-trees-talk
- Book Recommendation: Simard, Suzanne. "Finding the Mother Tree: Discovering the Wisdom of the Forest." *Knopf*, 2021. In this powerful memoir and scientific exploration, Simard uncovers the astonishing ways trees support one another, led by "mother trees" that act as the forest's central caregivers.

THE SECRET LIVES OF FUNGI: NATURE'S RECYCLERS

If fungi had a PR team, they'd be household names. These unsung heroes might not grab headlines, but they're absolutely essential to life on Earth. Fungi are the forest's cleanup crew, soil doctors, underground matchmakers, and even glow-in-the-dark performers.

Their superpower?

Decomposition. Fungi release enzymes that break down complex organic substances like cellulose and lignin (found in wood, leaves, and other plant material) into simpler molecules that other organisms can absorb. In doing so, fungi fuel the nutrient cycle and promote soil health. Without fungi, we'd be buried under mountains of dead leaves and fallen trees.

But fungi don't stop there. They're also collaborators. Through symbiotic relationships, fungi team up with plant roots to form a super-alliance. The fungi help plants absorb water and minerals from the soil. In return, the plants feed the fungi sugars from photosynthesis. It's a win-win with ancient roots. About 80% of land plants depend on it.

Still not impressed? Some fungi glow in the dark. Species like *Mycena chlorophos* emit an eerie green light, possibly to attract insects that spread their spores. Imagine tiny mushroom nightlights dotting the forest floor. Even in the dark, fungi find a way to be seen. It's both beautiful and a little spooky.

And let's not forget the superpowers of fungi in human innovation. The world's first antibiotic, penicillin, was born from mold. Today, fungi are used in bioremediation, cleaning up oil spills and toxic waste by breaking down pollutants. Fungi really know how to handle a mess.

Fungi might not wear capes, but make no mistake, they're the superheroes of the natural world.

Fascinating Facts

- Ecological Glue: Fungi are responsible for breaking down over 90% of all plant matter, making them essential to the carbon and nutrient cycles. The

world would not exist without fungi because plants would not be able to grow.
- Fungi are neither plants nor animals. They are in a kingdom of their own but are genetically much closer to animals.
- Biodiversity Giants: Scientists estimate there are between 2.2 and 3.8 million fungal species, but only about 150,000 have been formally identified.
- Medical Marvels: *Penicillium* fungi revolutionized medicine, saving millions of lives since the discovery of penicillin in 1928 by Alexander Fleming.

To Learn More

- Attenborough, David. "David Attenborough Encounters a Symbiotic Fungi!" *YouTube Nature Bites*, February 7, 2022. Join David Attenborough as he uncovers the astonishing symbiotic relationships fungi form with plants, revealing a hidden world beneath our feet. https://tinyurl.com/fungi-encounters
- BBC. "These fungi facts will blow your mind." *YouTube,* Feb 18, 2022. This quick, eye-opening video reveals bizarre and brilliant facts about fungi, from mind-controlling spores to planet-saving mushrooms. https://tinyurl.com/fungi-video
- Book recommendation: Sheldrake, Merlin. "Entangled Life: How Fungi Make Our Worlds, Change Our Minds & Shape Our Futures" *Random House*, May 2020. This captivating book delves into the mysterious and mind-bending world of fungi, revealing how these organisms connect ecosystems,

influence evolution, and challenge our understanding of life itself.

THE WEIGHT OF CLOUDS: A MILLION POUNDS OF FLOATING WATER

They may look like fluffy cotton candy drifting across the sky, but don't be fooled. Clouds are heavy. *Really heavy.* A typical cumulus cloud can weigh over a million pounds. That's about the weight of 100 elephants just hanging out overhead, floating along like it's no big deal.

Clouds are made up of billions of microscopic water droplets or ice crystals, each one barely a few microns wide. A micron is equal to one-millionth of a meter, or approximately 39 millionths of an inch. Yep, that's really tiny.

Even though each droplet is tiny, there are billions of them in a typical cumulus cloud. Add it all up, and you're looking at a staggering weight.

So why don't clouds fall? How does something that massive stay up there?

It all comes down to science and a little atmospheric magic. The air beneath clouds is even denser than the cloud itself. Warm air rises, carrying water vapor with it. As the vapor cools and condenses into droplets, it forms clouds. But because the tiny droplets remain spread out and lightweight, the cloud stays buoyant, floating in the sky instead of crashing down like a tidal wave.

Also, helping the cause? Updrafts. Those invisible currents of rising air give water droplets an extra lift. And because each droplet is so small, it falls so slowly that even a gentle breeze or updraft can keep it suspended. It's like nature's version of a slow-motion juggling act.

The next time you're lying on your back watching shapes drift by in the sky, remember: you're looking at a million-pound miracle.

Fascinating Facts

- Cloud Weight: A typical cumulus cloud can weigh over a million pounds yet still floats effortlessly. That's the equivalent of 100 adult elephants floating above your head.
- Water Content: Large storm clouds can contain billions of gallons of water—enough to fill thousands of swimming pools.
- Cloud Formation: Warm air rising creates low-pressure zones, allowing clouds to stay suspended instead of falling like rain.

To Learn More

- Rober, Mark. "How Much Do Clouds Actually Weigh?" *Science Channel YouTube,* February 17, 2016. This video breaks down the surprising science behind cloud weight and how they can weigh

millions of pounds. https://tinyurl.com/how-much-clouds-weigh-video
- Science Section, Library of Congress, Everyday Mysteries. "How Much Does a Cloud Weigh?" *Library of Congress*, October 27, 2023. This article explains how scientists calculate the staggering weight of clouds and why they still float effortlessly in the sky. https://tinyurl.com/how-much-clouds-weigh

NATURE'S DESERT SYMPHONY: SINGING SAND DUNES

In the scorching heat of the Namib Desert, located in Southwestern Africa, something utterly bizarre and spine-tingling happens: the sand sings. Not in melodies like birds or wind but with a deep, low hum that can echo for miles. This eerie natural sound, sometimes compared to the drone of a distant airplane or an organ note, is caused by a fascinating phenomenon known as "booming sand" or "singing dunes."

Welcome to one of nature's weirdest performances: the mysterious world of booming dunes.

So, how on Earth does a mountain of sand make sound? Why does a pile of dry sand belt out bass notes like it's auditioning for a desert symphony? Turns out, it's not magic. It's granular physics. When the conditions are just right (dry sand, uniform grains, a steep dune face, and a little nudge), the grains begin to cascade downhill in unison. As they rub and bounce against one another, they create synchronized vibrations. Think of it as the desert's version of a tuning fork, except made of billions of grains of sand jostling each other into harmony.

And Namibia isn't the only place where the sand gets musical. You can also find booming dunes in Morocco, Chile, China, and Kazakhstan. Even the good ol' U.S. of A. has singing sand dunes like Sand Mountain in Nevada and the Kelso Dunes in California's Mojave Desert. Each dune has its own tone and personality, as if Mother Nature is running a planet-wide music festival, no instruments required.

Dr. Nathalie Vriend of the University of Cambridge has spent years studying these musical mounds. Her research reveals that each dune has its own unique "voice," determined by the size of the grains and the shape of the dune. Some vibrate at low, thunderous frequencies; others produce higher-pitched murmurs. It's like every dune has its own playlist, one that only kicks in when you shake things up a bit. Some experts believe the sound comes from friction-induced vibrations between grains. Others think the entire dune acts like a massive speaker, resonating at its own acoustic frequency. Either way, it's a science with serious flair.

Of course, long before scientists started analyzing dune acoustics, people had their own theories. For centuries, local legends in desert regions spoke of the sands whispering secrets, echoing ancient chants, or carrying the voices of gods. In many cultures, the booming sound was believed to be supernatural: a warning, a sign, or a message from the beyond. It's a reminder that when nature makes noise, human imagination starts to hum along.

Today, we know it's all thanks to friction, vibration, and a little desert choreography. But standing at the edge of a massive dune as it rumbles beneath your feet? It still feels magical. Because sometimes, even when science explains the how, the *wow* remains.

Fascinating Facts

- The World's Oldest Desert: Namib is the world's oldest desert. It has been dry for at least 55 million years.
- Global Phenomenon: Singing dunes can be found in 35 desert locations worldwide, each producing its own distinct tone based on sand composition and dune shape.
- Scientific Insight: Research on granular flow helps improve safety in industries such as agriculture and construction, where flowing particles (like grains or sand) can create hazardous vibrations or structural stress.

To Learn More

- Fischer, Shannon. "Singing Sand Dunes Explained." *National Geographic*, October 21, 2012. This article explores the strange science behind why some sand dunes emit eerie, low-pitched "songs" when sand moves across their surface. https://tinyurl.com/singing-sand-dunes-explained

- "Uncovering the Mystery of Singing Sand Dunes." *One Minute Explore YouTube,* April 16, 2023. This excellent video opens with the music of a singing sand dune and then explains how friction, grain size, and motion combine to make sand dunes "sing" in the desert wind. https://tinyurl.com/singing-sand-dunes-video
- Williams, Barrett. "The Singing Sands: Unveiling the Phenomenon of Booming Dunes." *Audible Audiobook,* April 21, 2024. This engaging audiobook dives into the physics and folklore of singing sand dunes, revealing how nature's desert landscapes create spontaneous musical performances.

THE MAGIC OF BIOLUMINESCENT WATERS

You dip an oar into the inky black sea, and the sea suddenly comes alive. Each splash, swirl, or gentle wave lights up the water with an ethereal blue-green glow. This is bioluminescence, one of nature's most dazzling light shows, and it's performed nightly by millions of microscopic organisms.

The magic happens through a chemical reaction inside marine life, most commonly from dinoflagellates, which are tiny planktonic organisms. When disturbed by motion (like a paddle, a swimming fish, or a curious snorkeler), they unleash a chemical reaction. This chemical reaction creates a brief but brilliant burst of natural light. Think of it as nature's version of a glow stick: biodegradable, self-powered, and spectacular.

But these little glow-makers aren't just here to impress us. Bioluminescence is their defense system. Some flash to startle predators or light up their attackers for even bigger threats to see, like shouting, *"Hey! Look over here!"* Others, like the eerie deep-sea anglerfish, use bioluminescence as bait to lure dinner straight into their waiting jaws. In the dark ocean depths, it's glow or be eaten.

If you're itching to witness this ethereal glow, Mosquito Bay in Puerto Rico should top your list. Recognized by Guinness World Records as the brightest bioluminescent bay in the world, Mosquito Bay boasts up to 2.1 million dinoflagellates per gallon of water. The bay glows like liquid fire when night falls, and every movement in the water sparkles. The bay's unique geography, surrounded by mangroves and shielded from light pollution, creates the perfect environment for these organisms to thrive. Interestingly, after Hurricane María in 2017, scientists were stunned to find the glow actually intensified, with dinoflagellate numbers mysteriously doubling.

Halfway across the globe, Toyama Bay in Japan offers a different shade of wonder with glowing squid. Every spring, from March to June, millions of firefly squid ascend from the deep sea to spawn. These tiny creatures, about three inches long, are equipped with specialized light-producing organs called photophores, which emit a brilliant blue light. The result? A coastline awash in an ethereal glow. Locals and tourists line the shore to watch the water shimmer with an electric blue hue as if Mother Nature had decided to vacation in Japan.

So, if you ever find yourself near a bioluminescent bay, resist the urge to snap a photo and leave. Pause. Soak it in. Watch the water pulse with life. You're witnessing one of the planet's most mesmerizing natural miracles.

Fascinating Facts

- Brightest Glow: Mosquito Bay, Puerto Rico, was declared the world's brightest bioluminescent bay by Guinness World Records in 2006. The best time to visit is during the dry season, from December to mid-April.
- Glowing Life: Over 700 marine species use bioluminescence, including jellyfish, squid, plankton, and deep-sea fish.
- Fragile Ecosystem: A single motorboat or chemical pollutant can disrupt the chemical balance and reduce bioluminescent visibility for weeks.
- Relatively Rare: Bioluminescent bays require very specific conditions, including a very high concentration of dinoflagellates, which makes them relatively rare.

To Learn More

- Graham, Adam H. "Japan's mysterious glowing squid." *BBC Travel*, February 24, 2022. This article reveals the dazzling spectacle of Japan's firefly squid, tiny marine creatures that put on a glowing

underwater performance each spring. https://tinyurl.com/glowing-squid
- Matt Miller Film. "Bio Bays in Puerto Rico – Everything you need to know!" *Vos Travel with Kids. YouTube*, January 24, 2025. This family-friendly video gives a vibrant overview of Puerto Rico's glowing bays, explaining the science, history, and magic behind these natural light shows. https://tinyurl.com/bio-bays-video
- Nalewicki, Jennifer. "Puerto Rico's Bioluminescent Bays Are Brighter Than Ever." *Smithsonian Magazine Travel*. April 6, 2022. This article highlights how Puerto Rico's glowing bioluminescent bays have become even more radiant in recent years. https://tinyurl.com/brighter-bio-bays

FROZEN AND SPINNING: THE ICE DISCS THAT DANCE IN RIVERS

You're walking along a riverbank in the dead of winter when something catches your eye. In the middle of the icy water floats what looks like a giant, spinning coin—perfectly round, graceful, and slowly rotating in place. No wires. No trickery. Just an enormous disc of ice, twirling like nature's own vinyl record.

These mesmerizing formations are known as spinning ice circles, and they're one of winter's strangest and most elegant surprises. First documented in scientific literature in the 1890s, they continue to amaze researchers and passersby alike to this day.

So, how does this chilly magic happen?

It starts when freezing temperatures meet a slow-moving river or stream. As the air gets colder, a thin layer of ice forms on the water's surface. Occasionally, a small chunk breaks off. Instead of drifting away aimlessly, it catches the movement of small swirling eddies that form in the river's currents. These eddies gently begin to spin the chunk of ice, much like a potter's wheel spinning a lump of clay.

As the disc spins, it brushes against other pieces of ice and slushy water around it. This constant rotation grinds and smooths the edges, shaping it into an uncannily perfect circle. The motion is surprisingly steady, and the result is an icy sculpture created entirely by the interplay of physics and persistence.

The technical name for this effect is vortex-induced rotation. It's the same kind of motion that makes whirlpools spin or leaves dance in the corner of a windy street.

These icy wonders have appeared in rivers all over the world, such as the Sheyenne River in North Dakota and the River Otti in Norway. In 2019, the Presumpscot River in Maine had one spectacular disc reach nearly 300 feet wide, which drew international media attention.

Viral videos of these spinning circles frequently circulate on social media, captivating viewers worldwide. It's easy to see why they capture the public imagination; there's something almost magical about watching a massive ice disc spin with such elegance. While the physics may be complex, the result is a simple and beautiful display of nature's ability to surprise and enchant us.

Fascinating Facts

- First Recorded Sighting: The earliest known recorded ice circle was spotted in 1895 in the Mianus River in New York.
- Global Sightings: Ice circles have been observed in countries including the United States, Canada, Sweden, and Norway, typically during the coldest months.
- Perfect Conditions: Ice discs form best when air temperatures hover near freezing, water currents are slow, and the surface temperature gradient is stable.

To Learn More

- Cole, Brendan. "Physicists Have Finally Figured Out Why These Massive Ice Discs Start Spinning on Their Own." *Science Alert*, March 30, 2016. This article, including videos, explains the physics behind naturally spinning ice discs. https://tinyurl.com/why-ice-discs-spin
- Borneman, Elizabeth. "Ice Circles." *Geography Realm*, February 27, 2019. This informative article examines the formation and distribution of ice circles. https://tinyurl.com/ice-circles
- Science Channel. "This is How Nature Produces Perfect Ice Discs." *YouTube*, December 30, 2016. This short video shows how slow currents, cold temperatures, and precise conditions work together

to create nearly perfect spinning ice discs.
https://tinyurl.com/ice-discs-video

THE SCALE OF THE UNIVERSE: BEYOND IMAGINATION

If you ever want to feel truly humbled and just a little bit dizzy, try wrapping your brain around the scale of the universe. It's not just big. It's *absurdly big*. So big that words like immense, infinite, and mind-blowing start to feel like understatements. We live in a cosmos where some particles are so small that they make atoms look like beachballs, and some structures are so enormous that they make entire galaxies seem like specks of glitter on a black velvet canvas. The universe stretches in both directions: smaller than you can imagine, bigger than you can dream.

Let's start on the microscopic end of the cosmic scale. At the bottom of reality's size chart are particles like quarks, electrons, and neutrinos. They are so tiny that billions of them could fit on the period at the end of this sentence.

Zooming out (by many, many orders of magnitude), we reach familiar territory: cells, bugs, people, buildings, and planets. Earth feels big when you're flying coast to coast, but in astronomical terms, it's a pebble. The Sun is over a million times larger by volume. And the Sun itself? Just your average Joe among an estimated 100 to 400 billion stars in the Milky Way Galaxy.

Here's where things get wild. The Milky Way is a sprawling spiral of stars, gas, and dust that spans approximately 100,000 light-years. And yet, it's just one member of the Laniakea Supercluster, a local gathering of galaxies that spans 500 million light-years. We haven't even mentioned the heavyweights.

Say hello to IC 1101, one of the largest known galaxies in the universe. This elliptical behemoth spans up to 550,000 light-years from end to end. If you hopped in a spaceship moving at the speed of light, you'd still be soaring through it for more than half a million years. It's nearly five times the diameter of our galaxy. And that's not even the punchline because IC 1101 is just *one* galaxy. There are *two trillion* more!

To navigate these cosmic distances, astronomers use the light-year, which is the distance light travels in one Earth year, or approximately 5.88 trillion miles (9.46 trillion kilometers). And yet, even light (the fastest thing in the universe) takes 4.24 years to reach us from our nearest stellar neighbor, Proxima Centauri. That twinkling star you saw last night? Its light may have started its journey when you were still in elementary school. Many of the stars visible to the naked eye have been shining their light our way for hundreds or even thousands of years. Some of them may no longer exist.

You are peering into a universe so enormous that it's literally beyond imagination. Helping us peek into this vast cosmic ocean are high-tech marvels like the James Webb Space Telescope. Its gold-plated mirrors can spot galaxies over 13 billion light-years away, capturing the faint glow of the early universe not long after the Big Bang. In a sense, it lets us look back in time. You're time-traveling, eye-to-eye with the past.

Contemplating the universe's scale is a philosophical gut check. It stirs something ancient and curious in us. It challenges our understanding of time, distance, and significance. And it invites us to marvel at the unlikely miracle that we're here at all, on this pale blue dot, trying to measure the immeasurable.

Fascinating Facts

- Tiny Building Blocks: A typical hydrogen atom has a diameter of about 0.1 nanometers. A human hair is roughly 1 million times thicker.
- Mind-blowing Numbers: Over one million Earths could fit inside our Sun. The Sun is just one of 100 to 400 billion stars in the Milky Way. The Milky Way is just one of the 2 trillion galaxies in the universe.
- Largest Known Galaxy: IC 1101 is one of the largest known galaxies, spanning over 5.5 million light-years, or about 55 times the size of the Milky Way.
- Age of Universe: The universe is currently estimated to be 13.8 billion years old.

To Learn More

- "Scale of the Universe"- This interactive tool lets you zoom from the tiniest particles to the largest galaxies, offering a mind-bending tour of the universe's vast and hidden scales. https://scaleofuniverse.com/en

- Hofeldt, Alex. "How small are we in the scale of the universe?" *TED-Ed YouTube*, February 13, 2017. This animated TED-Ed video puts human size in cosmic perspective, exploring just how tiny we are in the grand scheme of the universe. https://tinyurl.com/how-small-we-are
- Zuckerman, Catherine. "Hidden world of microscopic life revealed in extraordinary pictures." *National Geographic*, February 8, 2019. Stunning close-up images reveal the beauty and complexity of the microscopic world that exists just beyond our naked eye. https://tinyurl.com/microscopic-life-pics
- Book recommendation: Watzke, Megan and Arcand, Kimberly. "Magnitude: The Scale of the Universe." *Black Dog & Leventhal*, November 2017. This visually rich book takes readers on a breathtaking journey through the scales of the universe, from subatomic particles to galaxy clusters and everything in between.

THE FERMI PARADOX: WHERE IS EVERYBODY?

The universe is vast. We're talking about two trillion galaxies, each one bursting with hundreds of billions of stars. Zoom in and many of those stars have planets, some of which orbit in just the right "Goldilocks zone," where conditions might be not too hot, not too cold, but just right for life. With that many cosmic lottery tickets, the odds seem wildly in favor of intelligent life popping up elsewhere. Yet, despite decades of searching, we've found no definitive signs of alien civilizations.

So, where is everybody?

This cosmic head-scratcher is known as the Fermi Paradox, named after physicist Enrico Fermi, who reportedly posed the question over lunch one day in the 1950s: "If the universe is so big and old, and intelligent life is statistically likely, why haven't we seen a single sign of it?" Not a spaceship. Not a message. Not even a trace of ancient galactic graffiti.

For decades, scientists have tried to make sense of the silence. Some theories are hopeful, others not so much.

One idea? We're being deliberately avoided. Perhaps advanced alien civilizations are following a "prime directive," choosing not to interfere with primitive worlds (yes, we're the primitives in this scenario). They could be waiting for us to reach a certain level of maturity or just watching us like a cosmic reality show they're not quite ready to cancel.

Another theory is darker: civilizations destroy themselves. They may rise up, build incredible technology, and then wipe themselves out through war, AI rebellion, environmental disaster, or some unforeseen catastrophe yet to be imagined. If that's true, then the reason the galaxy is quiet might be that it's littered with the ruins of once-brilliant species.

Then there's the unnerving possibility of The Great Filter, a step in the evolution of intelligent life that's nearly impossible to survive. It could be behind us (yay, we're rare survivors!) or still ahead (gulp, buckle up). No one knows.

But it might explain why the stars aren't exactly brimming with cosmic chatter.

Some scientists suggest that we're just looking at it wrong. Maybe aliens don't use radio signals. Perhaps they communicate through quantum entanglement, neutrino beams, or some other method that we are not yet aware of. Or their messages are so advanced that we don't even recognize them as communication.

Another comforting theory? We're early. The universe is nearly 14 billion years old, but stars will continue to form for trillions more years. We might be part of the first intelligent generation to crawl onto the galactic stage, nervously looking around a mostly empty auditorium. Give it time. Perhaps the real party hasn't started yet.

Still, that hasn't stopped us from searching. Projects like SETI (Search for Extraterrestrial Intelligence) continue to sweep the sky with massive radio telescopes, listening for any whispers from the cosmos. We've scanned thousands of stars. So far, nothing definitive. But the silence makes the question even more powerful.

Is no one out there? Or are we simply not ready to hear them?

Until we get an answer (or that first unmistakable "ping" from the stars), the Fermi Paradox will remain one of the universe's greatest, most tantalizing mysteries. And maybe the loneliest one, too.

Fascinating Facts

- Exoplanet Discoveries: The Milky Way alone is estimated to contain between 100 and 400 billion

stars, many of which may have potentially habitable planets. The Kepler space telescope was NASA's first planet-hunting mission. During its nine-year mission, Deep Space revealed that our galaxy contains billions of hidden "exoplanets," which are promising places for life.
- SETI's Search: The SETI Institute has scanned over 42,000 stars for intelligent signals—but so far, no confirmed contact.
- Galactic Timescale: Our civilization has only been sending radio signals for about 125 years. This is a mere blink of an eye compared to the universe's 13.8-billion-year history.

To Learn More

- Cox, Brian. "Brian Cox Explains the Fermi Paradox." *Science Time YouTube,* March 8, 2025. This excellent video explores the Fermi Paradox and why, in a vast universe full of stars and planets, we have yet to encounter alien life. https://tinyurl.com/fermi-paradox-video
- SETI Institute. The SETI Institute leads the scientific search for extraterrestrial intelligence by scanning the cosmos for potential signals from advanced civilizations. https://www.seti.org
- Book Recommendation: Davies, Paul. "The Eerie Silence: Renewing Our Search for Alien Intelligence." *Houghton Mifflin Harcourt,* 2010. In this thought-provoking book, physicist Paul Davies reexamines humanity's quest to find alien life. He challenges our assumptions about where and how we should look.

QUANTUM ENTANGLEMENT: THE WEIRDEST LOVE STORY IN PHYSICS

Imagine breaking a cookie in half, tossing one piece to New York and the other to Tokyo. Now, twist your half clockwise —and instantly, the other piece in Tokyo twists counterclockwise. No matter how far apart they are, they're still mysteriously linked in perfect opposition.

No delay, no wires, no messages. That's quantum entanglement. And it's 100% real. Scientists have been scratching their heads (and rewriting physics textbooks) ever since.

At the core of this phenomenon are particles (teeny-tiny bits of matter like photons or electrons) that become so connected that they basically form a cosmic "bond." Once entangled, they act like a single entity, even if you fling them to opposite ends of the universe. Tweak one, and the other responds *immediately*. That's what makes it so weird.

Albert Einstein hated this idea. He famously called it *"spooky action at a distance"* because, according to classical physics, this kind of instant reaction across space just shouldn't happen. He was convinced there had to be some sneaky "hidden variable" behind the scenes. However, experiments led by physicists like John Bell and Alain Aspect in the late 20th century showed otherwise. No hidden wires, no cheat codes. Just quantum mechanics doing its spooky thing.

So, what's the point of all this entangled weirdness? *Oh, just the future of technology!*

Quantum entanglement is the driving force behind next-generation quantum computers. These are machines that perform calculations that would take regular computers billions of years to complete. It's also the secret sauce in quantum encryption, a communication system so secure that even the best hackers wouldn't stand a chance.

Even more mind-blowing? Physicists have already pulled off quantum teleportation. Not of people (sorry, Trekkies), but of quantum information transmitting the exact state of one particle to another, instantly and without moving a single atom. It's the beginning of what could someday become a quantum internet.

The strangest part? We still don't fully understand how it works. And yet, it does. Quantum entanglement is a reminder that the universe doesn't have to play by our rules. It has its own, far stranger playbook. One where information may be shared invisibly across space, where distance doesn't matter, and where particles behave more like psychic twins than independent dots.

Spooky? Definitely. Real? Undeniably. Mind-blowing? Absolutely.

Fascinating Facts

- Beyond Distance: Entangled particles have been observed to remain correlated even when separated by over 1,000 kilometers, with changes occurring instantly. However, it's not about sending information faster than light (they don't actually send information).

SCIENCE & NATURAL WONDERS | 65

- New Computing Technologies: Quantum computers, which use entangled particles, can potentially solve problems that are too complex for conventional computers.
- Nobel-Worthy Science: The 2022 Nobel Prize in Physics was awarded to three scientists—Alain Aspect, John Clauser, and Anton Zeilinger—for groundbreaking experiments proving the reality of quantum entanglement.

To Learn More

- Ash, Arvin. "Quantum Entanglement Explained - How does it really work?" *YouTube,* Jul 30, 2021. In this clear and engaging video, Arvin Ash breaks down the mysterious phenomenon of quantum entanglement, explaining how particles can remain connected across vast distances. https://tinyurl.com/quantum-entanglement-video
- Science Exchange. "What Is Entanglement and Why Is It Important?" *Caltech Science Exchange.* This article from Caltech demystifies quantum entanglement and explains why it's not just weird; it's essential to quantum computing, encryption, and teleportation. https://tinyurl.com/what-is-entanglement

3

MIND-BLOWING FACTS ABOUT HUMANS

Think you know your own body? Think again. Beneath your skin lies a world of strange quirks, hidden superpowers, and mind-bending abilities that science is still trying to unravel. Your body isn't just a machine. It's a marvel. From people who can taste colors to the incredible strength triggered by a surge of adrenaline, the human body is far more complex and fascinating than it appears. In this chapter, we'll explore the biological mysteries and unexpected talents that make humans one of nature's most astonishing creations. Get ready to see yourself in a whole new light. And spoiler alert: it's way weirder than you think.

THE MYSTERY OF PHANTOM LIMBS: WHEN THE BRAIN PLAYS GHOST

Your arm is gone, but it itches. Your foot's been amputated, but it's cramping like it ran a marathon. Welcome to one of the brain's eeriest tricks: phantom limb sensation. It's a bizarre, unsettling, and, at times, painfully real experience where amputees continue to feel the presence of missing body parts. Sometimes, it's just a subtle tingle; other times, it's a sharp, stabbing pain.

So, what's going on?

While it sounds like something out of a ghost story, the real explanation lies in the tangled wiring of the brain. You see, the brain doesn't just forget a limb once it's gone. It has spent a lifetime getting signals from that arm or leg, and it's not ready to move on. Inside the sensory cortex (the brain's command center for touch), the map of your body still includes that missing part. When the real-world input stops, the brain fills in the gaps. That's why you might feel your toes wiggle even when there's no foot to wiggle them with. This phenomenon is a powerful reminder that the body and brain are deeply interconnected and that perception doesn't always depend on physical reality.

Sometimes, the brain takes it even further. Instead of just feeling the ghost of a hand, you feel it clench, curl, or convulse in pain. Yes, phantom limbs can experience pain, including sharp pain.

That's where scientists like Dr. Vilayanur Ramachandran stepped in with one of the most elegantly simple solutions in neuroscience: mirror therapy. By placing a mirror beside the existing limb, patients see a reflection that looks like the missing one. For some, the illusion is powerful enough to relieve their phantom pain. It's like tricking the brain into believing everything's back in place, and suddenly, the clenched ghost hand starts to relax.

Today, technology is giving the mirror box a sci-fi upgrade. Virtual reality systems now allow amputees to control digital versions of their lost limbs, giving their brains a much-needed visual fix. Studies have shown that these high-tech illusions can help reduce pain.

It turns out that the brain is a total pushover for a good illusion. Studies show that when the brain is tricked with mirrors or high-tech virtual reality, it not only reduces the pain but also starts acting as if the missing limb is back in place. The brain falls for it every time. But here's the twist: not everyone finds phantom limbs distressing. Some amputees find comfort in the sensation, as if part of them is still there, refusing to disappear. Others, though, live with intense and persistent pain that resists every treatment thrown at it. These stories, so varied and deeply personal, remind us that the mind and body don't always agree on what's real.

Whether it's an arm that won't stop itching or a leg that still wants to run, phantom limbs show us just how mysterious and powerful our brains really are. The body might be missing something, but the brain? The brain keeps playing its greatest hits on repeat.

Fascinating Facts

- Phantom Limb: A physician named Silas Weir Mitchell coined the phrase "Phantom Limb" in 1871.
- Prevalence: 80% or more of amputees report experiencing phantom limb sensations, many within days of amputation. Phantom sensations are not limited to limbs; they can also occur after the removal of other body parts.
- Mirror Therapy Works: In clinical studies, mirror therapy has been shown to reduce phantom limb pain in a significant number of patients.

To Learn More

- Cheriyedath, Susha. "What is a Phantom Limb." *News Medical Life & Sciences*, May 6, 2021. This article explains how and why people continue to feel sensations, including pain, in limbs that have been amputated https://tinyurl.com/what-is-a-phantom-limb
- Plethrons. "Phantom Limbs Explained." *YouTube,* March 23, 2015. This short video explains the science behind phantom limbs and how the brain's body map plays a key role in this puzzling experience. https://tinyurl.com/phantom-limb-video

SUPERHUMAN STRENGTH: ADRENALINE AND YOUR INNER SUPERPOWER

You've probably heard the story: a parent lifts a car to save a trapped child. It sounds like a scene from a superhero movie, but these rare bursts of strength are very real, and they come courtesy of a hormone called adrenaline.

When your brain senses extreme danger, it doesn't pause to write a to-do list. It hits the panic button and shouts a biological "GO!" That signal races to your adrenal glands, which immediately flood your bloodstream with adrenaline and its sidekick, cortisol. The result? Your body is primed to either fight or flee with surprising power.

This biological turbo boost can unleash the strength you never knew you had. Suddenly, you're not just you. You become a faster, sharper version of yourself. Your heart races, your breathing gets deeper, and your eyes widen to catch every detail. Blood rushes to your muscles, supercharging them for one mission: *survival*. Hidden muscle fibers, ones you normally don't use, are unleashed. It's as if your muscles had a secret reserve tank, and someone just hit the switch.

This biological power-up enables people to achieve those jaw-dropping acts of strength under stress. Scientists call it "hysterical strength," but don't let the name fool you. It's dead serious and well-documented. You're basically becoming your own emergency superhero, with adrenaline as your cape.

Athletes also experience adrenaline spikes during competition, helping them reach peak performance. But unlike in emergencies, they train to manage and control the rush.

But every superhero needs a cooldown. Adrenaline is meant for short bursts, not a lifestyle. If you keep hammering that panic button day after day, your body pays the price. Chronic stress can lead to anxiety, heart issues, and immune problems.

So yes, adrenaline can help you lift a car, outrun danger, or slam dunk your fear. Just don't rely on it to get through Monday mornings.

Fascinating Facts

- Hysterical Strength: An adrenaline rush is also referred to as "hysterical strength," a phenomenon where individuals display extraordinary strength during extreme stress. It is not officially recognized by the medical community because it is difficult to reproduce.
- Actual Examples: In 2006, a 41-year-old mother living in a remote Quebec village fought off a polar bear to protect her two sons. In 2019, Zac Clark, a 16-year-old high school football player from Butler, Ohio, lifted the front of a car off his neighbor who had become trapped when the car's jack failed.
- Stress Aftermath: Chronic exposure to adrenaline can contribute to anxiety, high blood pressure, and sleep disorders.

To Learn More

- Austin, Daryl. "Hysterical strength? Fight or Flight? This is how your body reacts to extreme stress." *National Geographic, Science*. March 19, 2024. This article explores the science behind hysterical strength and how the fight-or-flight response can unleash superhuman power in moments of extreme stress. https://tinyurl.com/hysterical-strength
- King, Lori. "What to Know about an Adrenaline Rush." *WebMD,* October 23, 2024. WebMD breaks down what happens in your body during an adrenaline rush, from increased heart rate to a sudden surge of strength and alertness. https://tinyurl.com/adrenaline-rush-info
- BuzzFeed Multiplayer. "How Strong Can an Adrenaline Rush Make You?" *YouTube,* January 1, 2018. This video examines real-life cases and scientific theories behind the remarkable strength a person can achieve when adrenaline kicks in. https://tinyurl.com/adrenaline-rush-video

THE SCIENCE OF SYNESTHESIA: SEEING SOUNDS AND TASTING COLORS

Imagine hearing a musical note and instantly seeing a splash of color. Or tasting a food and involuntarily picturing a shape. Welcome to the wild and wonderful world of synesthesia, a rare neurological condition where the senses aren't just working overtime. They're throwing a full-on sensory party.

For the lucky 4% of people with synesthesia, the brain doesn't just process sights, sounds, smells, or tastes one at a time. Instead, it throws a multisensory block party, where one trigger, such as a sound, invites other senses to join in the fun. A trumpet blast might light up in blue. A word might taste like lemon meringue. Some people even claim to "feel" shapes when they listen to music. Yep, it's as surreal and awesome as it sounds.

And this isn't just a matter of poetic flair. These experiences are involuntary, automatic, and highly consistent. A synesthete who associates the letter "A" with the color red will likely always perceive it as red.

So, what's behind this sensory superpower?

Scientists believe synesthesia results from increased crosstalk between the sensory regions in the brain. In most people, these areas are functionally separate. However, individuals with synesthesia have extra neural connections between regions responsible for processing different senses, or their brains may simply be less inhibited about sharing signals. This can cause sensory signals to activate multiple areas of the brain at the same time.

There are over 80 known types of synesthesia, including color-hearing, taste-shape associations, and even emotion-sensation blends, such as sadness feeling like sandpaper.

It's not considered a disorder. Quite the opposite. Artists and writers say it enhances their creativity, giving them a multi-sensory palette that most people can only dream of. Many synesthetes describe their condition as a gift. Musicians like Pharrell Williams and Billy Joel have spoken publicly about drawing inspiration from their synesthetic experiences to influence their music. For them, making music isn't just about sound. It's about color, movement, and even taste.

Synesthesia often runs in families, suggesting a genetic link. Diagnosing it can be tricky. There's no brain scan or blood test for it yet. Instead, scientists use long-term consistency tests, such as checking if someone consistently sees the letter "A" as red, even years later. Genuine synesthetes don't change their answers. Why would they? For them, that yellow 7 is just as real as your morning coffee.

Synesthesia might just be the brain's way of showing off, turning numbers into personalities and music into a light show. It's a thrilling reminder of just how flexible, bizarre, and beautiful the human brain can be.

Fascinating Facts

- Common Types: The most common form is grapheme-color synesthesia, where letters or numbers evoke specific colors.
- Runs in Families: Synesthesia is believed to have a genetic basis, often appearing in multiple generations.
- Often Unnoticed: About 4% of people experience some form of synesthesia, but it often goes unnoticed because it feels normal to those who have it.

- Enhanced Memory: Synesthesia is linked to enhanced memory—many synesthetes recall information more vividly due to their multisensory connections.

To Learn More

- Be Smart. "The Weird Reason Some People Can Taste Colors." *YouTube*, December 30, 2024. This well-done video delves into the science of synesthesia, exploring how some people experience the world in vivid, overlapping senses. https://tinyurl.com/synesthesia-video
- "Synesthesia." *Cleveland Clinic*, May 3, 2023. This medical overview explains the different types of synesthesia and how the brain creates unusual sensory crossovers, like hearing colors or feeling sounds. https://tinyurl.com/synesthesia-overview
- Book recommendation: Cytowic, R. E., & Eagleman, D. M. "Wednesday is Indigo Blue: Discovering the Brain of Synesthesia." *MIT Press*, September 30, 2011. This groundbreaking book explores the fascinating world of synesthesia, where senses merge, like tasting words or seeing music, and reveals what it teaches us about the human brain.

THE INCREDIBLE REGENERATIVE POWERS OF THE HUMAN LIVER

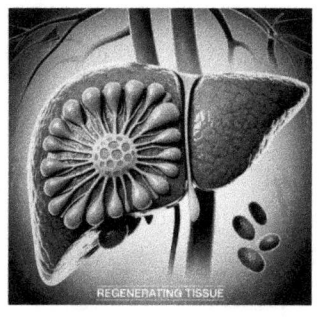

The liver is a bit of a show-off when it comes to regeneration. Slice it, dice it, take away up to 75% of its mass, and the liver simply shrugs, rolls up its sleeves, and starts growing right back. It's the only internal organ in the human body with true regenerative powers, and it doesn't just heal. It regenerates. It rebuilds! Functionally. Structurally. Like nothing ever happened.

At the heart of this miracle lies an army of highly specialized liver cells called hepatocytes. These microscopic workhorses aren't just sitting around processing toxins and storing nutrients. They are on call 24/7, ready to multiply like crazy the moment damage is detected. Think of them as construction workers who don't wait for permits. They get right to work the moment they sense trouble.

When injury strikes or part of the liver is surgically removed (a process called hepatectomy), the organ kicks off a cascade of molecular events. Chemical messengers, such as cytokines and growth factors, flood the area, triggering hepatocytes to enter overdrive. Within days, the liver can start replacing lost tissue, restoring both its size and function. That's key. It doesn't just grow back a lump of cells. It regenerates the exact architecture it needs to do its job: filtering toxins, producing bile, managing cholesterol, storing vitamins, and regulating blood chemistry.

Even more impressive? This happens without the need for stem cells in most cases. The liver mainly uses mature cells that can re-enter the cell cycle and divide, a rare talent in the world of organs. But in more severe cases, progenitor cells and stem-like cells may join the effort, filling in for damaged tissue when the usual players are overwhelmed.

That's why living-donor liver transplants are possible. Surgeons can remove part of a healthy person's liver and transplant it into someone else. Both livers grow back into full-functioning organs within just a matter of weeks or months. It's one of the only transplant scenarios where the donor can literally grow back what they gave away. However, factors such as existing liver conditions, age, lifestyle choices, and nutritional status can significantly impact this regeneration process.

The implications are enormous. If scientists can figure out how to trigger or mimic this regenerative process in people with liver failure or diseases like cirrhosis, it could be a game-changer. Researchers are already exploring ways to stimulate regeneration using gene therapy, cell-based treatments, and even bioengineered tissue scaffolds.

And just in case you thought ancient myths didn't know what they were talking about, think again. Apparently, the Greeks had a sense of biology. In the legend of Prometheus, the Titan was chained to a rock while an eagle feasted on his liver every single day. Each night, it grew back. Eternal torment? Sure. But is it biologically plausible? Surprisingly yes.

Fascinating Facts

- Regrowth Rate: The liver can regrow up to 75% of its mass within months after surgical removal or injury, restoring full function.
- No Scar Tissue: Unlike other organs, the liver's regeneration doesn't produce scar tissue, making it unique in its healing process.
- Mimicking Regeneration: Scientists are exploring ways to replicate liver regeneration, aiming to develop treatments for chronic liver diseases.

To Learn More

- "10 Marvelous Facts About Liver Regeneration." *Know It,* March 18, 2025. This brief video highlights surprising facts about the liver's remarkable ability to regenerate—even after major damage or surgical removal. https://tinyurl.com/liver-regeneration-video
- Jividen, Sarah. "Does the Liver Regenerate (and When Doesn't It)?" *Very Well Health,* January 6, 2025. This article explains how and when the liver can regenerate itself, as well as the conditions that can interfere with its healing powers. https://tinyurl.com/how-and-when-liver-regenerates
- "Liver regeneration." *Wikipedia.* A comprehensive look at the biological processes behind liver regeneration, including the science, mechanisms, and medical relevance of this vital organ's unique ability. https://tinyurl.com/wikipedia-liver-regeneration

THE ASTONISHING ABILITIES OF SUPERTASTERS

Ever feel like your salad is out to get you? Or that kale is trying to stage a coup on your taste buds? If so, you might just be a supertaster, part of an elite group of flavor warriors whose tongues experience the culinary world in ultra-high definition. It's a full-blown sensory explosion.

Thanks to a genetic variation, supertasters have significantly more taste buds than the average person: up to 1100 per square centimeter of the tongue, compared to around 100–400 in non-tasters. That means they perceive flavors more intensely, especially bitterness. What feels like a pleasant zing to most of us can hit a supertaster like a sour, bitter slap in the mouth. A simple Brussels sprout becomes a miniature bitter bomb. Coffee? A potential crime scene. Hoppy beer? Forget it.

The real culprit is a bitter chemical called PROP (*6-n-propylthiouracil*). To most people, it has a mild taste or is totally flavorless. To a supertaster, it's like licking a soap-soaked battery. Scientists use it to diagnose this flavorful superpower.

But being a supertaster isn't always a culinary superpower. Many steer clear of strong bitter foods (like kale, coffee, dark chocolate, and hoppy beers) not because they're picky but because those flavors are amplified to an almost painful degree. Ironically, this super sense can lead to less adventurous eating and even nutritional challenges when supertasters avoid healthy greens that taste like garden poison to them.

On the flip side, this sensory upgrade can be a ticket to flavor fame. Supertasters often excel in careers such as wine tasting, tea evaluation, or food science, where nuanced flavors are crucial. Their hypersensitive tongues can pick up on subtle differences the rest of us barely notice.

Approximately 25% of the population are considered supertasters, and this trait appears more frequently in women and individuals of Asian ancestry. Scientists believe this gene variation may have once been a survival tool. Bitterness often signals toxins in nature, so a sharp aversion might have helped early humans avoid eating something lethal.

So, is being a supertaster a blessing or a bitter curse? That depends. If you love bold flavors, it might feel like sensory overload. But if you enjoy decoding the hidden notes in a glass of wine or spotting the subtle zest in a perfectly crafted dish, your taste buds might just be your secret weapon.

Fascinating Facts

- % of Supertasters: About 25% of people are classified as supertasters, while the rest are either medium-tasters or non-tasters.
- Taste Bud Count: Supertasters have more than 30 taste buds per square centimeter of tongue, compared to fewer than 15 in non-tasters.
- Genetic Basis: Sensitivity to PROP is associated with variations in the TAS2R38 gene, which influences bitter taste perception. Women are more likely to be

supertasters than men, possibly due to genetic differences in taste sensitivity.

To Learn More

- BBC Earth Science. "Finding the Super Tasters" *YouTube,* July 26, 2019. This well-done video explores the world of supertasters and how their heightened senses shape what they eat and enjoy. https://tinyurl.com/supertasters-video
- Crosby, Guy. "Supertasters and Non-Tasters: Is it Better to Be Average?" *Harvard, The Nutrition Source,* May 31, 2016. This article examines the pros and cons of being a supertaster, non-taster, or somewhere in between—and what it means for your health and food choices. https://tinyurl.com/supertasters-pros-and-cons
- Holland, Kimberly. "Are You a Supertaster?" *Healthline,* February 21, 2019. Learn how to tell if you're a supertaster, what that means for your diet, and why some foods might taste more intense—or downright unpleasant—to you. https://tinyurl.com/how-to-tell-a-supertaster

THE SCIENCE BEHIND GOOSEBUMPS, YAWNING, AND OTHER BODY QUIRKS

Ever feel a chill, and suddenly, your skin turns into a patchwork of tiny bumps? Or find yourself yawning just because someone else did, even if you're wide awake? These odd little reflexes might seem random, but they're actually ancient leftovers from our evolutionary past.

Let's start with goosebumps. You know the feeling. Maybe your playlist hits that emotional crescendo, or a sudden breeze sends a chill across your skin, and boom! Your skin erupts into a patch of tiny bumps. These bumps happen when teeny muscles called arrector pili at the base of each hair follicle contract. Back in caveman days (when body hair was still "in"), this would fluff up fur for warmth or make you look bigger to scare off saber-toothed tigers. Today? It just makes you look extra dramatic during sad movie scenes, and we respect that. However, emotionally triggered goosebumps remain a mystery. Scientists believe it may be linked to the brain's reward system and the release of dopamine, which adds a physical shiver to an emotional high.

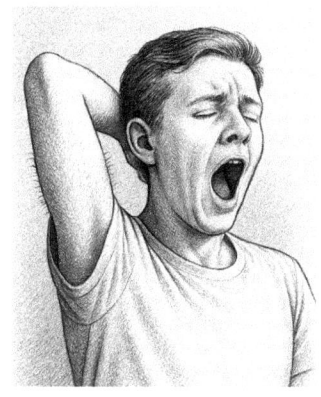

And what about yawning? No, it's not just your body's way of yelling, *"I'm bored!"* In fact, yawning may have more to do with brain temperature than boredom. Studies suggest that it helps cool the brain, acting like a mini air conditioner for your head. It boosts blood flow and draws in cool air, helping to keep your brain sharp and focused. Even weirder? Yawning is contagious. Watching someone yawn or even reading about it (yep, sorry!) can make you yawn too. Evolutionary psychologists believe this could be a leftover social bonding behavior from early human tribes, syncing everyone's alertness levels as a group.

And then we have the hiccup: the ninja of bodily functions. It sneaks up on you, strikes without warning, and leaves you hic-hic-hic'ing in public with zero dignity. A hiccup is a sudden spasm of your diaphragm, followed by your vocal cords slamming shut like a trapdoor. Scientists aren't entirely sure why we hiccup. One theory traces it back to our amphibian ancestors, who used similar movements to breathe underwater. Another theory? It helps babies release extra air while nursing. But truth be told, the hiccup hasn't revealed all its secrets. For now, it's still one of biology's quirkiest question marks.

So, the next time your body hits you with goosebumps during a killer song, yawns during a meeting, or drops a hiccup mid-sentence, just smile and remember: you're walking around with millions of years of evolution baked into your reflexes. And some of them are delightfully weird.

Fascinating Facts

- Goosebumps as an evolutionary leftover: When our hairy ancestors felt cold or threatened, their body hair would stand up to trap heat or make them look bigger to predators. These days, all we get is the chill and the tiny bumps.
- Hiccups aren't just for humans: Hiccups seem to occur in most mammals, including cats, rats, rabbits, horses, dogs, and humans.
- Social yawning: Just seeing or hearing someone yawn (or even thinking about yawning) can set off a yawn of your own. Strangely enough, many people feel more mellow and at ease right after they do it.

MIND-BLOWING FACTS ABOUT HUMANS | 85

To Learn More

- NPR's Skunk Bear. "Why Do We Get Goose Bumps?" *YouTube*, October 30,2015. This animated video uncovers the evolutionary roots of goosebumps, revealing why our skin still reacts like a startled porcupine. https://tinyurl.com/goosebumps-video
- Borunda, Alejandra. "The ongoing mystery of hiccups." *National Geographic Science*, April 5, 2023. Explore the quirky evolutionary theory that hiccups are a leftover reflex from our ancient, gill-breathing ancestors. https://tinyurl.com/mystery-of-hiccups
- Gatta, Frances. "Why Do We Yawn?" *WebMD*, March 15, 2024. This article investigates the possible reasons we yawn—from cooling the brain to syncing with those around us. https://tinyurl.com/why-we-yawn

THE MYSTERIES OF SLEEP PARALYSIS

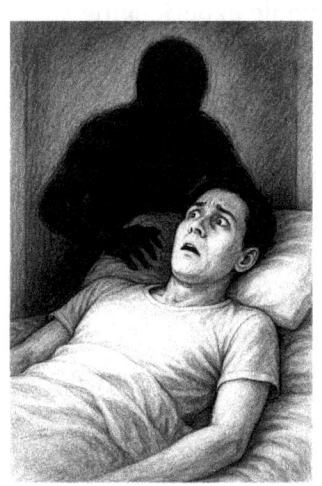

Imagine waking up in the dark, wide-eyed and alert, yet completely paralyzed. You try to move, but your limbs won't budge. You want to scream, but your voice is trapped somewhere between your lungs and lips. To make matters worse, you feel something watching you, maybe even pressing down on your chest like an invisible weight. Is it a nightmare? A ghost? A glitch in the Matrix?

Nope. Welcome to the eerie world of sleep paralysis, a real neurological phenomenon that's haunted humans for centuries—and inspired some of the creepiest legends on record.

Sleep paralysis occurs when your mind suddenly awakens during rapid eye movement (REM) sleep. REM is the phase when your brain is most active, and your dreams are the most vivid. During REM, your body naturally "locks down" your muscles, a feature called muscle atonia. It's a built-in safety feature designed to keep you from acting out your dreams (which would be dangerous for you and your bedroom furniture). Usually, your brain and body wake up in sync. However, sometimes, the brain activates the "wake" switch before the body does. When this happens, it leaves you in a bizarre limbo where you're fully conscious but still in lockdown mode. The result? You're awake and stuck. The experience can feel terrifying.

Now, here's where it gets bizarre. People experiencing sleep paralysis often report terrifying hallucinations, seeing ghostly figures, hearing whispers, and even feeling like something is sitting on their chest. These aren't just spooky stories. They're rooted in how your brain tries to make sense of being alert in a body that can't move.

No wonder this phenomenon has inspired chilling folklore worldwide. In Newfoundland, they blame the Old Hag, a witch-like figure who sits on your chest. In Japan, it's Kanashibari, meaning "bound in metal," often attributed to spirits or angry ancestors. Even in ancient Rome, people blamed nighttime demons called incubi for the terrifying sensation. In the U.S.? We tend to go with aliens, naturally.

But science has offered clarity. Sleep paralysis is usually harmless, just incredibly freaky. It's often triggered by things like stress, sleep deprivation, irregular sleep schedules, jet lag, or narcolepsy. Think of it as your body's weird way of saying, *"Hey, get some rest!"*

The next time you find yourself wide awake and unable to move, don't panic. It's a temporary misfire. You're not haunted. And the spooky stuff? That's your mind's attempt to fill in the blanks. Terrifying? Maybe. Fascinating? Absolutely.

Fascinating Facts

- Timing Trouble: Sleep paralysis typically occurs during transitions in or out of REM sleep, when muscle atonia is still active but consciousness returns. An episode is temporary and only lasts for a few seconds to a couple of minutes.
- Global Phenomenon: Studies estimate that 8–30% of people experience sleep paralysis at least once in their lives, often starting in the teen years. Certain sleep positions, such as lying on one's back, may increase the likelihood of experiencing episodes of sleep paralysis.
- Not Just a Dream: About 75% of sleep paralysis episodes include hallucinations, often involving pressure on the chest or sensing an "intruder."

To Learn More

- Sleep Is the Foundation. "Sleep Paralysis: What You Need to Know!" *YouTube,* November 1, 2022. This video explains the causes and sensations of sleep paralysis, including why you might feel trapped or see vivid hallucinations during episodes. https://tinyurl.com/sleep-paralysis-video
- "Sleep Paralysis." *Cleveland Clinic Health Library,* 07/03/2024. This medical guide covers what sleep paralysis is, who's most affected, and how to manage or prevent this unsettling sleep disorder. https://tinyurl.com/sleep-paralysis-overview
- Book recommendation: Popiashvili, Giorgi. "Prisoners of sleep: Face to face with sleep paralysis. This personal and scientific exploration of sleep paralysis dives into its terrifying realities and offers insight into coping with this mysterious condition. *Independently Published*, February 13, 2025

THE LIMITS OF ENDURANCE: HUMAN BODY EXTREMES

Think you're tough? Try running 350 miles without sleep, climbing an icy mountain in your underwear, or free-soloing a 3,000-foot vertical rock face with nothing but your fingertips and pure nerve. These aren't action movie stunts. They're real-life feats accomplished by human beings who have pushed their endurance to the edge of what seems biologically possible.

Take Dean Karnazes, nicknamed the "Ultramarathon Man." He once ran 50 marathons in 50 states in 50 consecutive days. *No, that's not a typo.* Even more jaw-dropping, he has been documented as running 350 miles straight without sleep. His muscles seem to bypass the usual "I quit" signals most of us get after a few hours. How? Scientists believe Karnazes has an ultra-efficient metabolism and an extraordinary ability to flush out lactic acid, the stuff that turns your legs into jelly during normal workouts. Meanwhile, his mental toughness is off the charts. He doesn't just run through pain; he high-fives it on the way by.

And then there's Wim Hof, better known as "The Iceman," who treats freezing temperatures like a spa day. This guy has run a half marathon barefoot in the snow above the Arctic Circle, sat in a tub of ice for nearly two hours, and climbed parts of Mount Everest in shorts and sneakers. His secret weapon? The Wim Hof Method, a mix of cold exposure, breath control, and meditation. This combo helps him tap into his autonomic nervous system like a human thermostat. Researchers were so intrigued that they studied his immune response. It also turns out he can voluntarily trigger adrenaline surges that would normally require life-threatening danger to activate.

Endurance isn't only about miles or ice baths. Sometimes, it's about defying gravity and fear itself. Enter Alex Honnold, the daredevil climber who scaled Yosemite's El Capitan without a rope. That's 3,000 feet of sheer granite, climbed with nothing more than chalk, shoes, and a terrifying amount of self-control. One slip, and it would have been a fatal plunge. Scientists scanned Honnold's brain and discovered something remarkable: his amygdala, the part responsible for fear, barely reacts to stimuli that would send most people into panic mode. In other words, he's not fearless. He just doesn't get rattled like the rest of us.

These people are outliers, but they reveal something extraordinary about human biology. When stress hits, the body has a hidden "turbo mode." Under extreme conditions, we can activate untapped muscle fibers, suppress pain, and push our systems far beyond normal limits.

However, there's a catch: this comes at a cost. Chronic stress, overtraining, and adrenaline overload can damage the heart, wear down joints, and wreck the immune system. It's like burning rocket fuel in a lawnmower: great for takeoff, terrible for longevity.

Still, these stories prove one thing beyond a shadow of a doubt. When body and mind are in sync, humans can achieve remarkable feats. We may not all be ultramarathoners or icemen, but the endurance lurking within us is greater than we often imagine.

Fascinating Facts

- Muscle Adaptation: Ultramarathon runners can develop mitochondria-rich muscles that burn fat and clear lactic acid more efficiently, enabling them to

run continuously for over 100 miles under extreme conditions.
- Cold Tolerance: Wim Hof has maintained his core temperature in subzero conditions, demonstrating that trained breathing and circulation control can override typical cold responses, once thought to be impossible.
- Mental Training: Free solo climbers train their brains to suppress fear, using visualization techniques to manage adrenaline during dangerous climbs.

To Learn More

- Nat Geo Live. "Free Soloing with Alex Honnold." *National Geographic,* August 29, 2011. Watch legendary climber Alex Honnold recount his mind-blowing free solo ascents, scaling sheer cliffs without ropes, fear, or margin for error. https://tinyurl.com/alex-honnold-video
- Uproxx Life Human Limits. "Dean Karnazes: The Ultramarathon Man." *YouTube,* September 18, 2017. This video profiles Dean Karnazes, the man who pushes human endurance to the limit by running hundreds of miles without sleep or stopping. https://tinyurl.com/Dean-Karnazes-video
- Uproxx Life Human Limits. "Wim Hof, The Iceman Cometh." *YouTube,* Sep 26, 2016. Discover how Wim Hof defies cold and logic using breathwork, mindset, and extreme exposure—earning him the nickname "The Iceman." https://tinyurl.com/Wim-Hof-video

EPIC JOURNEYS UNDERTAKEN BY INDIVIDUALS

Some people take the scenic route. Others rewrite history with it.

Imagine trekking across deserts, braving icy mountains, or flying solo across oceans. No GPS, no autopilot, and no streaming playlist to keep you company. The world's boldest explorers have proven that epic journeys are real, grueling, and utterly awe-inspiring. From ancient trade routes to global circumnavigation, epic human journeys have tested the limits of human endurance, innovation, and curiosity for centuries.

Let's start with Marco Polo. In the late 13th century, at the age of 17, he embarked on a 24-year journey with his father and uncle, which took him from Venice to China. A journey spanning over 15,000 miles across the Silk Road. No tour buses. No snack bars. Just months on horseback, camelback, and sometimes foot, documenting the cultures and riches of the East in ways that shaped European exploration for generations. He served in the court of Kublai Khan and returned home to Europe with stories so incredible that many Europeans thought he made the whole thing up. His travels opened up East-West exchanges that changed global trade and curiosity forever.

Fast forward to the age of aviation and meet Amelia Earhart: fearless, trailblazing, and flying headfirst into history. In 1932, she became the first woman to fly solo across the

Atlantic Ocean. Just her and the clouds. She endured 15 hours of storms, mechanical issues, and exhaustion to land in Ireland. Her transatlantic solo flight was a groundbreaking feat in aviation history, showcasing advances in airplane technology that made long-haul flights possible. But Earhart wasn't finished. Her 1937 attempt to circumnavigate the globe ended in mystery. However, it cemented her legacy as an aviation pioneer and icon of perseverance that still inspires.

Think that's impressive? Wait till you meet Erik Weihenmayer, whose journey redefined what it means to explore the limits of the human spirit. Despite losing his sight at the age of 13 due to a rare eye disease, Erik didn't just adapt; he climbed even higher. In 2001, he became the first blind person to reach the summit of Mount Everest. But he didn't stop there. Over the next decade, he scaled *all* Seven Summits, the highest peaks on each continent. This is a feat that only a select few sighted climbers have achieved. Erik's expeditions prove that vision isn't limited to what we see. It's about the determination to push past what seems impossible. His journeys inspire not only admiration for his physical endurance but awe at his mental resilience and the expanding definition of exploration. He's living proof that vision isn't about what you see. It's about what you believe you can do.

And, of course, there's Neil Armstrong, who didn't just journey around the world; he left it entirely. In 1969, aboard Apollo 11, Armstrong traveled over 238,000 miles from Earth to become the first human to set foot on the lunar surface. With his famous words, *"That's one small step for man, one giant leap for mankind,"* he didn't just mark a technological triumph. His moonwalk symbolized a new frontier, proving that the human desire to reach beyond known limits doesn't stop at the edge of our world.

These extraordinary journeys weren't just about distance. They were about the discovery of new lands, new frontiers, and the full, ferocious power of the human spirit. They remind us that the bravest paths are often the ones that no one has taken before. They're proof that with enough passion, perseverance, and possibly jet fuel, there's no limit to where we can go.

Fascinating Facts

- Marco Polo Journey: Marco Polo's journey lasted over 24 years and covered an estimated 15,000 round trip along the Silk Road.
- Amelia Earhart's Solo Flight: Amelia Earhart's solo Atlantic flight in 1932 took 15 hours, making her the first woman to cross the Atlantic alone.
- Climbing Mount Everest blind: In 2001, Eric Weihenmayer became the first blind person to climb Mount Everest and later all Seven Summits, challenging conventional notions of human limits.
- Neil Armstrong's trip to the Moon: The journey covered nearly 500,000 miles round trip (from Earth to the Moon and back), marking the first human journey beyond Earth in 1969.

To Learn More

- "Amelia Earhart." *National Air and Space Museum, Smithsonian.* This Smithsonian profile celebrates the

daring life and legacy of Amelia Earhart, an aviation pioneer and fearless trailblazer in the skies. https://tinyurl.com/amelia-earhart-profile
- PBS. "Marco Polo". *PBS Learning Media*. This video explores the life of Marco Polo and his epic journey to Asia. https://tinyurl.com/Marco-Polo-PBS-Video
- NASA History. "July 20, 1969: One Giant Leap for Mankind." *NASA*. July 20, 2019. NASA's documentation, including videos of the moon landing, including Armstrong's famous quote and flight details. https://tinyurl.com/armstrong-moon-landing
- Today NBC News. "Meet Erik Weihenmayer: The Blind Adventurer Who Conquered Mount Everest and Grand Canyon." *YouTube*, July 24, 2017. NBC episode about Erik Weihenmayer, who, despite being blind, summited Mount Everest and kayaked the entire length of the Grand Canyon. https://tinyurl.com/erik-weihenmayer-video

4

HISTORICAL ODDITIES

Think history is all dusty dates and boring battles? Think again. The past is brimming with stories that are bizarre, absurd, and jaw-droppingly weird. In this chapter, we'll track down entire colonies that disappeared without a clue, witness beer barrels detonating with explosive force, and sit in on a courtroom drama where a dead pope was put on trial (*yes, really*.) These aren't legends or tall tales. They're real events, pulled straight from the annals of history. They prove that the truth is not only stranger than fiction; it's way more entertaining. So, grab your historical passport and prepare for a ride through the past you definitely weren't expecting.

THE DANCING PLAGUE OF 1518

It's a sweltering July day in 1518. You're strolling through Strasbourg (then part of the Holy Roman Empire) when you stumble upon a strange scene: a woman in the middle of the street, dancing. No music. No audience. Just wild, flailing

 limbs and unrelenting rhythm. You shrug it off as one person's odd behavior, until others join in. Within days, dozens more follow. Within a month, the number swells into the hundreds. Somewhere between 50 and 400 people dance continuously for weeks.

They weren't partying. They were prisoners of their own bodies. Some collapsed from sheer exhaustion, and others suffered strokes or heart attacks. A few, according to accounts, quite literally danced themselves to death.

This wasn't a festival. It was a crisis. Known today as the Dancing Plague of 1518, this bizarre episode remains one of the strangest mass events in history. At the time, officials were baffled, and oddly enough, they thought the solution was more dancing. They believed this was some "hot blood" affliction that needed to be worked out of their systems. They brought in musicians and even constructed a stage to help "sweat it out." But this only made things worse and intensified the madness.

So, what was going on?

One popular theory blames ergot, a hallucinogenic mold that grows on damp rye and can cause convulsions and hallucinations. Ergot poisoning (known as ergotism) has been linked to strange behaviors throughout history. Still, skeptics point out that ergot typically causes seizures and death, not marathon dance sessions.

Another explanation is mass psychogenic illness (MPI), formerly known as mass hysteria. The people of 16th-century Strasbourg were deeply stressed. They faced famine, disease, poverty, and the looming shadow of divine punishment. In such a pressure cooker, the collective psyche may have cracked, expressing its torment through the universal language of dance. And because they believed it might be caused by spiritual possession or punishment by St. Vitus (the patron saint of dancing, oddly enough), the affliction spread like wildfire through fear and suggestion.

The dancing eventually stopped as mysteriously as it began. No one truly knows what sparked the frenzy or why it spread so wildly. Was it a neurological illness, a toxic exposure, or a powerful expression of collective trauma? Whatever the cause, the Dancing Plague of 1518 is one of history's strangest reminders that sometimes, when the body and mind are overwhelmed, even a dance floor can become a battleground.

Fascinating Facts

- A Deadly Dance: The "dancing plague" began with Frau Troffea, who danced for nearly a week. Within a month, 400 people were reportedly affected, with dozens dying from exhaustion, stroke, or heart attack.
- Hallucinations or Hysteria? Some scholars suggest ergot poisoning from moldy rye bread may have caused LSD-like effects. Others argue it was a case of mass hysteria rooted in trauma and fear.
- Curing Dance with Dance: Local leaders tried to solve the crisis by building a stage and hiring

musicians, hoping that music would help. Instead, it may have prolonged the chaos.

To Learn More

- Nick's Not Niche. "They DANCED till they DIED: The Dancing Plague of 1518." *YouTube*, May 30, 2023. This is an engaging video that transports viewers to Strasbourg, France, in 1518 during the infamous Dancing Plague. https://tinyurl.com/Dancing-Plague-Video
- Rosalind Jana. "The people who 'danced themselves to death,'" *BBC*, May 12, 2022. This article examines a chilling historical event in which a mysterious dancing mania swept through a medieval town, blurring the line between mass hysteria and medical mystery. https://tinyurl.com/BBC-Dancing-Plague
- Book recommendation: Waller, John. "The Dancing Plague: The Strange, True Story of an Extraordinary Illness." *Sourcebooks*, September 1, 2009. Historian John Waller investigates the bizarre 1518 outbreak that caused people to dance for days on end, revealing what it says about the human mind, society, and stress.

THE MYSTERY OF THE VOYNICH MANUSCRIPT

Imagine finding a book that resembles something out of a wizard's library, filled with strange drawings of alien-looking plants, mystical symbols, and women bathing in what appear to be magical hot tubs. The text? Written in an uncrackable code that has defied the world's best minds for

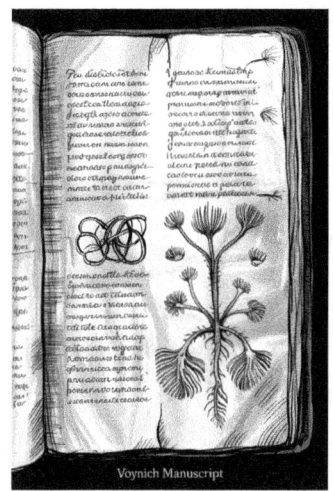
Voynich Manuscript

over 600 years. Welcome to the baffling, brain-teasing world of the Voynich Manuscript.

Discovered in 1912 by rare book dealer Wilfrid Voynich, this mysterious 240-page medieval manuscript, now housed at Yale University's Beinecke Rare Book & Manuscript Library, has captivated cryptographers, linguists, and historians alike. Radiocarbon dating places its creation between 1404 and 1438, but that's about the only thing we do know for sure.

No one knows who wrote it, why it was written, or what it's even saying.

Inside its pages are botanical illustrations of plants that don't exist (at least, not on this planet), astrological charts with zodiac symbols, and pages that seem to describe recipes or rituals. It's like a mix of a herbal guide, a horoscope, and a fever dream. Some say it's an ancient medicinal guide. Others claim it's a magical book of spells. A few believe it's just a 15th-century prank pulled off by a very bored monk with a calligraphy hobby. But every theory seems to create more questions than it answers.

And then there's the writing: an elegant, looping script dubbed "Voynichese" that doesn't match any known language, living or dead. Cryptographers from World War II, the NSA, and top universities have tried to break the code. And nothing. Its unique structure and statistical patterns suggest it could be a real language or an elaborate hoax.

Modern technology has entered the fray, with digital imaging and AI analysis attempting to unravel its secrets. These tools have revealed hidden details, adding new layers to the puzzle. For the world's best linguists, historians, and AI systems, the "Voynichese" language remains uncracked. The answers remain just out of reach, adding to the manuscript's irresistible allure.

So here we are, six centuries later, and we still have no idea who wrote it, what it says, or why anyone went to the trouble of making it look so important. But that's precisely why the Voynich Manuscript is so beloved. It doesn't just whisper secrets; it dares you to chase them. It's a centuries-old puzzle box that continues to spark wonder, wild theories, and just a hint of madness.

Fascinating Facts

- Found in a Jesuit College: The manuscript was rediscovered in 1912 by Wilfrid Voynich in a collection belonging to an old Jesuit college in Italy. Its journey before that is still a mystery.
- Undeciphered for Over 500 Years: Despite intense study, no one has been able to definitively decode the Voynich Manuscript's unique language—not even top cryptographers or AI models.
- Housed at Yale University:Since 1969, the manuscript has been housed in Yale's Beinecke Rare Book & Manuscript Library, cataloged as MS 408, and high-resolution scans of it can be viewed online.

To Learn More

- Dave Roos. "Why the Voynich Manuscript May Be the World's Most Mysterious Book." *History.com*, May 27, 2025. This article explores the enduring mystery of the Voynich Manuscript, a centuries-old book written in an undeciphered language that continues to baffle historians and codebreakers. https://tinyurl.com/voynich-manuscript-mystery
- "Voynich manuscript." *Wikipedia*. A comprehensive overview of the enigmatic Voynich Manuscript, covering its history, structure, illustrations, and the countless theories surrounding its origins and meaning. https://tinyurl.com/voynich-manuscript

THE LONDON BEER FLOOD: THE DAY ALE TOOK OVER THE STREETS

Forget about raging rivers or crashing waves. On October 17, 1814, London faced a very different kind of flood. Not of water, but beer. Dark, frothy, room-temperature porter, to be exact. It was a day when the city was hit with one of the strangest and sudsiest industrial disasters in history: The Great London Beer Flood.

It all started at Meux & Company's Horse Shoe Brewery on Tottenham Court Road, where enormous wooden vats held hundreds of thousands of gallons of porter (a popular dark beer at the time). These vats were enormous, some as tall as three-story buildings, and were held together by massive iron hoops. But on that fateful day, one of those hoops snapped. And then, disaster.

The ruptured vat exploded with a deafening roar, releasing a tidal surge of beer so powerful that it smashed through walls and triggered a chain reaction. Nearby vats couldn't handle the pressure, and they also burst. Within seconds, over 320,000 gallons of beer poured into the surrounding streets of St. Giles Rookery, one of London's poorest and most overcrowded slums.

This wasn't just a minor spill; it was a 15-foot-high tidal wave of ale cascading through homes, causing chaos and destruction. With no drainage on the city streets, the beer tore through walls, basements, and homes, tragically claiming eight lives, mostly women and children. Basements flooded. Houses collapsed. And while some accounts mention people trying to salvage beer in buckets, others describe a chaotic and heartbreaking scene. The recovery was grueling, with residents attempting to salvage what they could in a neighborhood already teetering on the edge of poverty.

Some accounts claimed that desperate locals tried to scoop up the beer in pots and pans. Others suggest looting, drunkenness, and public mourning with more than a hint of intoxication. The smell of stale beer lingered in the streets for months.

When the case went to court, the flood was ruled an *"Act of God,"* meaning Meux & Co. was off the hook for damages.

HISTORICAL ODDITIES | 105

There was no compensation for the victims or their families. The brewery continued production and even received a tax break to offset the losses.

By 1922, the brewery had closed and was torn down. Today, the Dominion Theatre now sits on part of the old site. Few passersby realize that beneath their feet lies the former epicenter of London's strangest natural disaster, one that literally poured through history.

The London Beer Flood is a surreal chapter in the city's past. It's a bizarre mix of tragedy and absurdity that proves even beer can become a force of destruction when things go terribly wrong.

Fascinating Facts

- A Vat the Size of a House.: The main vat was over 22 feet high and held the equivalent of 3,500 barrels or the equivalent of more than 1 million pints of beer—enough to keep a small town tipsy for a year!
- Eight Lives Lost: The flood tragically killed eight people, most of whom lived in the basement-level dwellings where the wave hit hardest.
- No One Was Held Accountable: Despite the destruction, the courts ruled that the event was an "act of God," thereby freeing the brewery from any legal or financial responsibility.

To Learn More

- History Thumbprint. "The Beer Flood of 1814." *YouTube*, March 13, 2024. This video dives into the

strange history of London's deadly beer disaster, where thousands of gallons of ale surged through the streets, flattening homes and shocking a city. https://tinyurl.com/beer-flood-video
- "The Time London Had a Beer Flood That Killed People." *EpicHistoryFacts.com*, March 8, 2025. Explore how a routine day at a brewery turned into one of history's strangest industrial accidents—with beer flooding the streets and claiming lives. https://tinyurl.com/beer-flood-that-killed-people

THE LOST CITY OF Z: ELUSIVE LEGENDS OF EXPLORATION

If you've ever dreamed of hacking your way through dense jungle vines in search of a hidden city, then you're in the company of one of history's most daring explorers: Colonel Percy Fawcett. Think Indiana Jones with a British accent and a real-life obsession.

Fawcett wasn't content with just the usual expeditions. He was obsessed with finding a mythical city he dubbed the "Lost City of Z." This wasn't just any city; it was rumored to be an advanced civilization of ancient wisdom hidden deep within the Amazon rainforest.

Fawcett's fascination was sparked by indigenous stories, old conquistador accounts, and mysterious artifacts. His earlier expeditions through South America had only fueled his belief. He encountered strange ruins, unexplained pottery, and native legends about vast cities that had been swallowed by the forest. Fawcett was hooked. The jungle wasn't just dangerous; it was keeping secrets.

In 1925, Fawcett embarked on what would be his most famous and final expedition, what he called "the Great Journey." He ventured into the Mato Grosso region of Brazil with his son, Jack, and Jack's friend Raleigh Rimell, determined to uncover the secrets of Z.

Then, silence. Fawcett and his crew disappeared without a trace. No distress signals, no bodies, no journals floated downstream. It was as if the jungle itself had swallowed them whole. The disappearance launched a century of rescue missions, conspiracy theories, and wild speculation. Were they killed by hostile tribes? Did they live out their days as jungle kings? Did they actually find Z?

The idea of Z captivated imaginations worldwide, with Fawcett's disappearance adding an air of mystery and romance to the legend. The tale became so compelling that bestselling author David Grann penned *The Lost City of Z* in 2009, a gripping blend of biography, history, and investigative journalism. The book rekindled public fascination and was later adapted into a lush, haunting film in 2016.

But here's the twist: the story may not have been just a jungle fantasy. Was Fawcett onto something all along?

Indigenous oral histories had long spoken of grand societies in the rainforest. These are stories of complex societies rich in culture and knowledge that were passed down through generations.

In recent years, satellite imaging and LIDAR (Light Detection and Ranging) technology have revealed geometric earthworks and hidden urban grids beneath the foliage: hints of large, complex societies that once flourished in the Amazon.

Historians had long dismissed the Amazon as too poor in nutrients to support civilization. However, it turns out that the ancient Amazonians may have engineered the soil, creating "terra preta," or dark earth, to sustain their agriculture. These weren't random tribes; they were planners, engineers, and city builders.

These findings suggest that sophisticated pre-Columbian societies may indeed have thrived in the Amazon, challenging our understanding of history and proving that, sometimes, legends hold a kernel of truth.

So, was Z real? Fawcett may have been chasing a legend, but that legend was rooted in truth. Maybe, just maybe, he was ahead of his time.

Fascinating Facts

- He Vanished in 1925: Fawcett's final letter from the field described crossing the Upper Xingu River—after that, nothing. No remains or confirmed sightings were ever found.
- LIDAR Reveals the Past: In the 21st century, LIDAR scans uncovered vast networks of roads, mounds, and settlements in the Amazon, proving the existence of complex, urban civilizations long before European contact.

- Hundreds Searched, Many Lost: Over the years, more than 100 people have died or gone missing trying to solve the mystery of Fawcett's fate or to find the fabled city themselves.

To Learn More

- Amazon Studios. "The Lost City of Z – David Grann Featurette." *Prime Movies,* April 15, 2017. This featurette explores the real-life inspiration behind the film "The Lost City of Z," blending historical adventure with David Grann's gripping research on a legendary Amazonian civilization. https://tinyurl.com/Lost-City-of-Z-video
- Handwerk, Brian. "Lost Cities of the Amazon Discovered From the Air." *Smithsonian Magazine,* May 25, 2022. Using cutting-edge aerial technology, researchers have uncovered long-hidden urban settlements in the Amazon, bringing new life to tales once dismissed as myth. https://tinyurl.com/lost-cities-of-the-amazon
- Book recommendation: Grann, David. "The Lost City of Z: A Tale of Deadly Obsession in the Amazon." *Vintage,* February 17, 2009. This thrilling nonfiction book chronicles the obsessive journey of British explorer Percy Fawcett as he searches for a fabled ancient city hidden deep within the Amazon rainforest.

THE DISAPPEARANCE OF THE ROANOKE COLONY

You set off on a bold adventure across the Atlantic to start a new life. You build homes, plant crops, and try to survive in unfamiliar territory. Then, poof! Your entire community vanishes. No smoke signals, no farewell notes, just one word carved into a wooden post: CROATOAN.

Welcome to America's oldest unsolved mystery: the centuries-old puzzle known as The Lost Colony of Roanoke.

In 1587, 115 English settlers landed on Roanoke Island, off the coast of what is now North Carolina. Led by Governor John White, they were England's second attempt to plant a permanent colony in the New World. The group included families, craftsmen, and even White's own daughter, Eleanor Dare, who gave birth to Virginia Dare, the first English child born in America.

However, their supplies soon ran low, and relations with the local tribes were strained. White sailed back to England for reinforcements. He expected to return in a few months, but Queen Elizabeth had other plans. England was locked in a naval war with Spain (hello, Spanish Armada), and every seaworthy vessel was seized for battle. White was stranded. It took three long years before White could return.

When he finally returned in 1590, what he found was chilling: no colony, no people, and no buildings. Just eerie silence. The fort was dismantled, not destroyed. The only clue? "CROATOAN" was carved into a wooden post, and "CRO" was etched into a tree nearby. The settlement was abandoned. No signs of struggle. Just that haunting clue: CROATOAN, the name of a nearby island and its native tribe.

Was it a clue? A farewell? A desperate message? Historians, archaeologists, and mystery enthusiasts have long been fascinated by these cryptic messages. Theories abound.

Did the colonists flee to Croatoan Island (now Hatteras Island) and merge with the local Croatan people? Were they attacked? Did they starve? Some suggest disease or harsh weather forced them to relocate inland. Others suspect a more tragic fate: disease, starvation, or simply death by wilderness. To this day, it's a mystery with no clear answers, only theories.

But wait, there's more.

Recent archaeological digs on Hatteras Island have uncovered European artifacts in Native American settlements, including nails, a sword hilt, and a writing slate. Coincidence? Or proof that the colonists lived on? Meanwhile, DNA researchers are hunting for genetic clues in local populations, hoping to find descendants of those long-lost pioneers. History meets CSI, with a side of time travel.

More than four centuries later, the Roanoke Colony remains a haunting riddle, a tale of hope, hardship, and historical vanishing acts. It's inspired novels, TV shows, horror stories, and legends. And still, we ask: What happened to the Lost Colony? Was "CROATOAN" a destination, a plea for help, or a final farewell carved into history?

Whatever the truth, the Lost Colony remains one of the greatest historical mysteries ever carved into a tree. And the eerie word "CROATOAN" still echoes through the fog of history like a ghostly whisper.

Fascinating Facts

- Only Clue: "CROATOAN": The word was found carved into a wooden post. No cross or distress signal was left, suggesting the settlers weren't taken by force.
- Governor White's Delay: White's return was postponed by the Anglo-Spanish War, delaying crucial supplies and support. By the time he got back, the colony had been gone for years.
- Modern Investigations: Recent digs on nearby Hatteras and Roanoke Islands have uncovered European artifacts, and DNA studies are underway to determine if today's local tribes share ancestry with the lost colonists.

To Learn More

- Incredible Stories. "The Lost Colony of Roanoke: One of America's Greatest Mysteries." *YouTube*, May 5, 2025. This video covers the enduring mystery of the Lost Colony of Roanoke, where over 100 settlers vanished without a trace. https://tinyurl.com/lost-colony-video
- Sci NC, PBS North Carolina. "New Clues to the Fate of the Lost Colony." *YouTube.* January 20, 2017. Explore the latest archaeological findings and

emerging theories that may finally shed light on what happened to the Roanoke colonists. https://tinyurl.com/lost-colony-new-clues-video
- Book recommendation: Lawler, Andrew. "The Secret Token: Myth, Obsession, and the Search for the Lost Colony of Roanoke." *Anchor,* June 4, 2019. Andrew Lawler weaves history, myth, and modern detective work into a gripping narrative about America's oldest unsolved mystery, the fate of the Lost Colony.

THE YEAR WITHOUT A SUMMER: 1816

Ever heard of a summer that never came? Imagine stepping outside in June expecting blue skies and sunshine, only to be greeted by snow. Chickens freezing solid, crops withering before they sprout, lakes frosting over in the middle of July. It sounds like the setup for an apocalyptic movie. But it really happened.

Welcome to the year 1816, famously dubbed "The Year Without a Summer," when the world's weather went completely off the rails thanks to one very angry volcano halfway around the world.

It all started the year before. In April 1815, Mount Tambora in Indonesia erupted with mind-blowing force. It was one of the most powerful volcanic eruptions in recorded history. The blast was so immense it could be heard more than 1,200 miles away. It launched over 36 cubic miles of ash, gas, and rock into the atmosphere and killed tens of thousands of people near the island. But Tambora wasn't done. Its ash cloud rode the wind currents high into the stratosphere. It circled the globe, acting like a giant sunshade and plunging global temperatures into a deep chill.

The result? Total atmospheric chaos. Across Europe and North America, snow fell in June. Frost touched crops in July. In August, lakes that should've been warm enough to swim in remained stubbornly icy. Farmers were forced to replant again and again, only to watch their efforts fail. Wheat and oat prices skyrocketed. In some places, people survived on acorns, moss, and boiled weeds. Riots broke out over food shortages. It wasn't just an agricultural crisis; it became a global humanitarian disaster. Social unrest bubbled up as hungry populations demanded solutions. The ripple effects of Tambora's fury were felt far and wide.

But even as misery spread, something remarkable was happening. In a cold, gray villa on the shores of Lake Geneva, Mary Shelley and her literary companions were trapped indoors, bored and freezing. So, they held a ghost story contest. Out of that dreary, lightless summer came Frankenstein, the world's first science fiction novel.

Meanwhile, the death of many horses due to starvation spurred a German inventor named Karl Drais to build a new method of transportation: the precursor to the modern bicycle.

Today, scientists cite 1816 as a classic example of how interconnected and vulnerable our planet really is. That ghostly summer stands as a chilling reminder that a single event, buried deep in the Earth, can cast a global shadow, unsettle empires, but at the same time ignite the kind of creativity and resilience that define what it means to be human."

As strange as it sounds, the eruption of a volcano no one in the West had even heard of managed to dim the sun, chill the planet, and alter the course of history.

Fascinating Facts

- A Blast Like No Other: Mount Tambora's 1815 eruption was the most powerful in over a thousand years (Volcanic Explosivity Index 7), releasing ash and gas high into the stratosphere. 10,000 people died immediately, and up to 90,000 in the after-effects.
- Snow in Summer: In 1816, parts of New England saw snow in June, with widespread frosts in July and August—crippling crops and causing food shortages. It is estimated that 1 million people died of famine worldwide.
- A Cold Spark of Inspiration: Stuck indoors during the gloomy summer, Mary Shelley began writing Frankenstein, a literary classic born from literal darkness. The lack of oats to feed horses inspired the German inventor Karl Drais to invent the velocipede, a precursor of the bicycle.

To Learn More

- Landrigan, Dan and Landrigan, Leslie." 1816: The Year Without a Summer." *New England Historical Society.* This article recounts how the volcanic

aftermath of Mount Tambora's eruption led to a year of bizarre weather, failed crops, and widespread hardship across New England and beyond. https://tinyurl.com/1816-year-without-a-summer
- OzGeology. "The Notorious 1815 Eruption of Mount Tambora." *YouTube*, November 1, 2023. This video explores the catastrophic 1815 eruption of Mount Tambora, one of the deadliest in history, and how it triggered global climate chaos. https://tinyurl.com/1815-eruption-video
- Book recommendation. Klingaman, William K. and Klingaman, Nicholas. "The Year Without Summer: 1816 and the Volcano That Darkened the World and Changed History." *St. Martin's Griffin*, March 11, 2014. This book offers a sweeping account of how one volcanic eruption plunged the world into darkness, disrupted societies, and reshaped history in the summer of 1816.

THE GREAT EMU WAR: AUSTRALIA'S FLIGHTLESS FOES

When you think of military history, machine guns, and battle tactics, you probably don't think of giant birds. But in 1932, Australia launched an official military operation against an unexpected adversary: the emus. Emus are those tall, flightless birds that can run up to 30 miles per hour and leap fences with ease.

Sometimes, the most absurd-sounding stories are absolutely true, and this one is legendary.

Welcome to 1932, deep in Western Australia, where returning World War I veterans were promised farmland to start fresh. But Mother Nature had other plans. The Great Depression hit hard, droughts plagued the land, and just when the wheat harvest looked salvageable – BAM! In came an unexpected enemy force: emus. Not just a few. We're talking an estimated 20,000 of them, migrating en masse and descending upon the fields like crop-crunching invaders.

Desperate farmers pleaded with the government for assistance. In response, the Ministry of Defence (that's the Australian spelling of 'defense') dispatched soldiers armed with Lewis machine guns. They were ready to teach these oversized birds a lesson. And so began one of the most bizarre battles in Australian history: The Great Emu War.

However, it turns out that the emus were natural guerrilla fighters. They didn't bunch together like polite targets. They scattered in swift, unpredictable sprints. They ran up to 50 km/h (about 30 mph), could pivot like ballerinas, and had an uncanny knack for dodging bullets.

Despite firing over 2,500 rounds, the soldiers only managed to take down around 1,000 birds. That's an ammo-to-bird ratio that would make any general weep. The operation was such a disaster that after just a few weeks (and significant media mockery), the government pulled the plug. The emus, undefeated, strutted off into the brush.

The aftermath? The press had a field day. The birds were deemed the victors of what was now mockingly referred to as a "war." Parliament faced public ridicule, and military officials swore never to involve the army in pest control again.

The Great Emu War has since become a symbol of both the unpredictability of nature and the unintended consequences of over-the-top solutions. In the end, the government abandoned the battle. This unusual chapter in history prompted a reevaluation of pest control strategies, shifting the focus toward more sustainable, non-military solutions like fencing and crop management to handle wildlife conflicts.

And while it may sound like an episode of Monty Python, the Great Emu War is 100% real. It remains a feathered footnote in history, a hilarious cautionary tale of what happens when you bring machine guns to a bird fight and forget that nature doesn't always follow orders.

Fascinating Facts

- A Bird-Brained Battle Plan: The military deployed soldiers with Lewis machine guns and thousands of rounds of ammunition, but the birds proved too fast and unpredictable to hit consistently.
- Emus: 1, Australia: 0: After weeks of failed operations, only a small fraction of emus were culled, prompting headlines that the birds had "won."
- From Bullets to Barriers: Following the failure, the government pivoted to non-military solutions to manage the impact of wildlife on crops.

To Learn More

- ABC Australia. "The Great Emu War: how it started and who won." *YouTube,* December 29, 2022. This video tells the bizarre true story of how Australia declared war on emus—and lost—after thousands of flightless birds overran farmland in 1932. https://tinyurl.com/emu-war-video
- Travers, Scott. "The Real Story Behind Australia's Great Emu' War' Of 1932 (And Why They Lost—Twice)." *Forbes.com*, December 26, 2024. This article explains the surreal military campaign against emus, revealing how the birds outsmarted soldiers twice and secured their place in quirky history. https://tinyurl.com/story-of-great-emu-war

THE MAN WHO SURVIVED TWO ATOMIC BOMBS

Let us introduce you to Tsutomu Yamaguchi, the only officially recognized person to survive both atomic bombings in Hiroshima and Nagasaki. *Yes, you read that right.* Not one nuclear explosion, but two, in the span of three unthinkable days. If ever there were a real-life embodiment of grit, fate, and the sheer will to live, this was it.

It all began on August 6, 1945. Yamaguchi, a 29-year-old engineer for Mitsubishi Heavy Industries, was in Hiroshima on a business trip when the first atomic bomb dropped. The sky lit up with a blinding flash, followed by a thunderous roar and a heat wave that turned the city into a smoldering inferno. He was less than two miles from ground zero. The blast ruptured his eardrums, left him with severe burns, and tossed him through the air like a rag doll. Dazed but alive, he stumbled his way to a shelter and spent the night in the shattered remains of the city.

The next day, because apparently surviving a nuclear explosion wasn't enough for one week, he made his way back to his hometown of Nagasaki. He reported for work (because, *of course*, he did), trying to explain to his bosses what he had just endured. They thought he was exaggerating. Then, on August 9, the second bomb exploded over Nagasaki. His office was blown apart, and the city was plunged into chaos. And Yamaguchi survived again.

His story would sound like fiction if it weren't so well-documented. Despite being severely injured and emotionally devastated, he lived to tell the tale. Even more incredible? He became a passionate advocate for nuclear disarmament, spending the rest of his life sharing his story to warn the world about the horrors of nuclear war. In 2009, the Japanese government officially recognized him as a double hibakusha, someone exposed to both atomic bombings.

Yamaguchi passed away in 2010 at the age of 93. His extraordinary story is a testament not only to the terrifying power of human warfare but also to the nearly unbreakable strength of the human spirit. Some called him the unluckiest man in history. Others, the luckiest. But he was something else altogether: the world's most resilient witness.

Fascinating Facts

- Double Hibakusha: Yamaguchi is the only person officially recognized by the Japanese government as a hibakusha (bombing survivor) of both Hiroshima and Nagasaki.
- Within 2 Miles—Twice: In Hiroshima, he was about 1.8 miles from the blast's epicenter; in Nagasaki, roughly the same distance. Surviving one atomic bomb at that range is rare. Surviving two? Practically unheard of.
- Peace Advocate: In his later years, Yamaguchi wrote books, gave interviews, and even appeared in a documentary to push for nuclear disarmament. It was his way of turning personal tragedy into global purpose.

To Learn More

- Andrews, Evan. "The Man Who Survived Two Atomic Bombs." *History.com.* This article tells the astonishing true story of Tsutomu Yamaguchi, the only officially recognized person to survive both the Hiroshima and Nagasaki atomic bombings. https://tinyurl.com/survived-two-atom-bombs
- History. "Amazing Survivor Lives Through Two Nuclear Explosions." *YouTube,* August 21, 2022. This video recounts the harrowing and inspiring tale of a man who endured the unthinkable: surviving not one but two nuclear attacks in 1945 Japan. https://tinyurl.com/survived-two-atom-bombs-video

- Book recommendation: Pellegrino, Charles. "To Hell and Back: The Last Train from Hiroshima." *Rowman & Littlefield Publishers*, February 7, 2019. This powerful book blends survivor accounts and historical insight to chronicle the devastation of the atomic bombings and the extraordinary resilience of those who lived through them.

THE CADAVER SYNOD: WHEN A POPE PUT A DEAD POPE ON TRIAL

Courtroom dramas typically involve fiery lawyers, scandalous accusations, and the occasional gasping jury. But in 897 AD, the Catholic Church added an unforgettable twist. The defendant was a rotting corpse.

Yes, you read that right.

In one of the most outrageous and macabre episodes in papal history, Pope Stephen VI decided he hadn't quite finished arguing with his predecessor, Pope Formosus. The minor detail that Formosus had been dead for nearly nine months didn't matter. Fueled by political rage and pressure from rival factions, Stephen VI exhumed the late pope's decaying body, dressed it in full papal regalia, sat it on a throne, and held what can only be described as a medieval horror show disguised as a trial.

This real-life zombie courtroom circus is known as the Cadaver Synod. And it was every bit as grotesque as it sounds.

The charges? A stew of medieval grievances: perjury, violating Church law by serving as a bishop outside his designated region, and improperly claiming the papacy. Essentially, Stephen VI was trying to erase Formosus from Church history. But watching a bloated, decomposing corpse "stand trial" while a poor deacon muttered in his defense? That pushed even the medieval Church's flair for ceremony into the territory of grotesque theater.

As the bloated corpse sat silently, the deacon awkwardly "defended" him. At the same time, onlookers watched the ghastly proceedings with shock and awe. The court found the corpse guilty, stripped it of its sacred vestments, and cut off the fingers Formosus had used to bless. And just to drive the point home, chucked his desecrated body into the Tiber River. Legend has it the corpse later washed ashore and began performing miracles.

But the twisted drama didn't end there. The grotesque trial sparked public outrage, and the backlash was swift. Pope Stephen VI's monstrous obsession with posthumous punishment shocked even the most jaded observers. Within months, Stephen was overthrown, imprisoned, and, according to most accounts, was strangled in his cell. The Church declared the Cadaver Synod null and void. Formosus was quietly reburied in St. Peter's Basilica.

But history doesn't forget. The Cadaver Synod stands as one of the strangest, darkest, and most theatrical political power plays ever staged. It's a reminder that, in some eras, not even death could save you from the perils of office politics.

Fascinating Facts

- A Corpse on Trial: Pope Formosus's body was physically exhumed, dressed in papal finery, and propped on a throne to face a full ecclesiastical trial nearly nine months after his death.
- Fingers of Judgment: The three fingers used for giving blessings were ceremonially severed, symbolically stripping Formosus of his spiritual authority.
- Backlash Was Swift: Public disgust led to Stephen VI's downfall. He was overthrown, imprisoned, and likely murdered. The Church reversed the trial's verdict and reburied Formosus with honor.

To Learn More:

- Harper, Elizabeth. "The Cadaver Synod: When a Pope's Corpse Was Put on Trial." *Atlas Obscura*, March 3, 2014. This article dives into one of history's most bizarre and macabre events when Pope Formosus's corpse was exhumed and placed on trial by the Catholic Church in 897. https://tinyurl.com/cadaver-synod
- Forgotten History. "Dead Pope on Trial: The Cadaver Synod." *YouTube*, May 28, 2025. This video

recounts the chilling spectacle of the Cadaver Synod, where church politics took a grotesque turn as a dead pope was tried, condemned, and thrown into the Tiber. https://tinyurl.com/cadaver-synod-video

5

EVERYDAY THINGS YOU DIDN'T KNOW HAD A SECRET HISTORY

You brush with it, sit on it, snack on it, flush it away, and maybe even nuke your leftovers in it. Yet, odds are, you've never once asked, *"Wait...who thought this up?"* Well, prepare to be delighted. Many of our most ordinary, everyday items at home and in medical offices around the world have backstories that are anything but boring. Some were total accidents. Others were the result of decades (or even centuries!) of tinkering, trial and error, and the occasional stroke of genius. In this chapter, we rip open the packaging on everything from sticky notes to cereal, toothbrushes to toilets, X-rays to penicillin, and discover the weird, wild, and wonderfully unexpected origins behind the stuff you use without a second thought. Get ready to appreciate everyday items as if they were a museum of bizarre brilliance.

GOING IN STYLE: THE STRANGE, CIVILIZING HISTORY OF TOILETS AND TP

Let's face it. Few inventions are more underappreciated than the toilet. It's not flashy. It's not fun to talk about at dinner parties. But this humble household fixture has done more to protect public health and human dignity than almost any other device in history. And paired with its trusty sidekick, toilet paper, it's a duo that deserves a standing ovation (or at least a clean seat).

But getting to the modern flush toilet was, well, a long and messy business.

In ancient Mesopotamia and the Indus Valley, people used clay-seated toilets connected to rudimentary drainage systems. Primitive, yes, but surprisingly efficient. The Greeks and Romans upped the game with communal latrines: long stone benches with holes arranged in neat rows. These were more social than sanitary, with flowing water underneath and shared sponge sticks soaked in vinegar. One stick per group. *We'll let that visual sink in.*

For centuries afterward, people turned to chamber pots, which were essentially indoor bowls you kept under the bed. You did your business, then emptied it into the street or the backyard. Chamber pots were used from the Middle Ages right up through the 1800s, especially in households without indoor plumbing. Often, they were beautifully decorated. Because if you're going to go, go in style.

In 1596, English courtier and poet Sir John Harington built the first known flushing toilet for Queen Elizabeth I. She wasn't too thrilled about using it, and the world wasn't ready to part with chamber pots just yet. Toilets wouldn't go mainstream for another 200 years.

The real splash came in the Victorian era when indoor plumbing finally started to creep into private homes. Enter Thomas Crapper (*yes, that's his real name*), a savvy London plumber who improved toilet design, patented several innovations, and ran a successful bathroom fixture business. Though he didn't invent the toilet, his name became legendary thanks to clever marketing, royal endorsements, and, let's be honest, the *perfectly fitting surname*.

And what of toilet paper? In 1857, American entrepreneur Joseph Gayetty introduced the first commercially packaged toilet paper, flat sheets infused with aloe and sold as a "medicated health aid." Still, many people stuck with familiar alternatives: catalogs, newspapers, leaves, and corncobs (*ouch*). TP didn't truly go mainstream until the 20th century when indoor plumbing demanded something that wouldn't clog the pipes.

But not everyone in the world uses toilet paper—nor do they want to.

In many countries, hygiene routines look different. Across parts of Asia, the Middle East, and Africa, people often use water instead of paper, using a small handheld water jug or a built-in spray hose. In Japan, bathrooms have gone from humble to high-tech. Modern Japanese toilets often come with heated seats, adjustable water sprays, air dryers, motion sensors, and even music to mask sound. Meanwhile, in

Europe and South America, bidets, once considered exotic, are standard in many homes.

In fact, many people argue that water is cleaner, more sustainable, and more comfortable than paper. And the global conversation about "the right way to wipe" is more passionate than you'd expect.

Fascinating Facts

- Crapper Was a Real Person: Thomas Crapper helped popularize modern plumbing and toilets in Victorian England. Though he didn't invent the toilet, his name is now forever linked to bathroom lore.
- Toilet Paper Took Time to Catch On: The first rolls were considered a luxury, and even in the 1930s, some brands proudly advertised their paper as "splinter-free."
- Japan's Toilets Are Next-Level: Some Japanese "smart toilets" offer heated seats, automatic lids, rear and front bidet sprays, deodorizers, dryers, and even built-in music players.
- Toilets Save Lives: Modern sanitation, including toilets, has been one of the most important public health advances, helping to dramatically reduce the spread of disease worldwide.

To Learn More:

- Weird History. "The History of Toilets." *YouTube*, January 12, 2020. This video takes a humorous yet informative look at the evolution of toilets—from

ancient latrines to modern plumbing marvels. https://tinyurl.com/history-of-toilets-video
- History at Home. "The Remarkable History of Toilet Paper." *YouTube*, April 27, 2020. Discover the surprising and quirky history of toilet paper in this video, which traces its path from ancient alternatives to the rolls we rely on today. https://tinyurl.com/history-of-toilet-paper-video

X-RAYS: THE INVISIBLE DISCOVERY THAT CHANGED MEDICINE

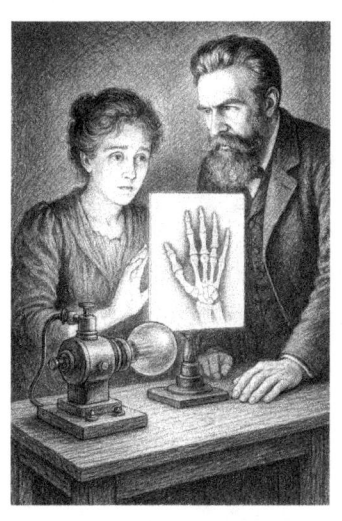

It was a regular November evening in 1895. German physicist Wilhelm Conrad Röntgen was tinkering in his lab, probably not expecting to accidentally revolutionize modern medicine. He was experimenting with cathode rays, those invisible beams produced in vacuum tubes. He wrapped his apparatus in black cardboard to block the visible light. That should've been the end of it. But then something strange happened. A fluorescent screen sitting nearby suddenly began to glow, even though no light was supposed to escape. So, what was lighting it up?

Naturally, Röntgen did what any good scientist would do: he placed a variety of objects in front of the tube and the glowing screen. Books. Metal. Wood. They all cast strange shadows, and he could see right through them.

Finally, he asked his wife, Bertha, to place her hand in front of the screen. What he saw next was the shadowy outline of her bones and her wedding ring glowing back at him. Bertha, understandably, was horrified. She allegedly exclaimed, *"I have seen my own death!"* (Whether she really said that or it's the stuff of scientific legend, we may never know.)

But Wilhelm knew what he had seen wasn't death. They had seen something else entirely. He had stumbled upon a mysterious new kind of ray. He called them "X-rays" (*X* for 'unknown') because he had no clue what they were. And despite having no formal medical training, Röntgen had just opened a literal window into the human body. X-rays were born.

Within *weeks*, the world pounced on this breakthrough. Doctors were peering inside patients without cutting them open. Bullets lodged in bodies? No longer a mystery. Fractured bones? Suddenly crystal clear. It was medicine's equivalent of turning on the lights. No waiting for decades of peer-reviewed research or FDA approval or double-blind trials. Just *"Here's the machine; let's see what it does!"*

By 1901, Röntgen had earned the first-ever Nobel Prize in Physics, cementing his legacy as the man who gave humanity its first peek into the invisible. And in a move as noble as the prize itself, Röntgen refused to patent his discovery. He believed something this important should belong to the world. That's right, while others were cashing in on the

Industrial Age, Röntgen gave away the blueprint for one of the most powerful diagnostic tools in history.

Today, X-rays are the unsung heroes of hospitals, dentist chairs, airports, and even art museums. But it all began with one curious scientist, a glowing screen, and a very surprised wife.

Fascinating Facts

- A Hand in History: The first X-ray image ever taken was of Röntgen's wife's hand, showing her bones and wedding ring. It was described as both ghostly and groundbreaking.
- The "X" Still Means Mystery: Röntgen called them X-rays because he didn't know what the rays were. Today, we know they're part of the electromagnetic spectrum, just beyond ultraviolet.
- Fastest Medical Adoption in History: Within weeks of the discovery, X-rays were being used in surgery, diagnostics, and even by the military to locate bullets in wounded soldiers.

To Learn More

- APS Advancing Physics. "November 8, 1895: Roentgen's Discovery of X-Rays." *APS News*, November 1, 2002. This article recounts how Wilhelm Roentgen accidentally discovered X-rays in 1895, revolutionizing medicine and earning the first Nobel Prize in Physics. https://tinyurl.com/discovery-of-xrays

- Mediphysman. "Discovery of the Xray." *YouTube*, June 27, 2024. This informative video explains how a glowing screen and scientific curiosity led Roentgen to uncover the invisible rays that changed diagnostic science forever. https://tinyurl.com/discovery-of-xrays-video
- Book recommendation. Berger, Harold. "The Mystery of a New Kind of Rays: The Story of Wilhelm Conrad Roentgen and His Discovery of X-Rays." *CreateSpace Independent Publishing*, September 6, 2012. This engaging book tells the story of Wilhelm Roentgen's groundbreaking discovery of X-rays and how it reshaped the worlds of physics and medicine.

MICROWAVE OVENS: A MELTED CANDY BAR CHANGED THE KITCHEN

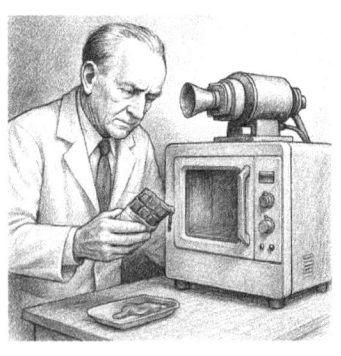

In the grand hall of accidental brilliance, the invention of the microwave oven deserves its own standing ovation and perhaps a snack. This everyday kitchen hero wasn't born from a love of cooking but from military radar experiments and a gooey, melting candy bar.

The year was 1945. World War II had just ended, and Percy Spencer, a self-taught engineer with a knack for tinkering, was deep into research at Raytheon, a company developing radar systems. One day, while fine-tuning a magnetron (a device that emits microwaves), Spencer noticed something odd. The chocolate bar in his pocket had mysteriously melted. Most of us would mourn the loss of a perfectly good candy bar. But Percy? He saw potential. Curious and excited, he wondered if the microwaves from the device had something to do with it.

Spencer wasted no time testing his theory. He grabbed a bag of popcorn kernels and placed them near the magnetron. Seconds later, pop! They exploded into fluffy white popcorn and scattered across the room. Next, he tried an egg, but the rapid heating caused it to explode in the face of an observing colleague. Messy, yes. But undeniable proof that microwaves can cook food!

Realizing he'd stumbled onto something extraordinary, Spencer and Raytheon quickly got to work. By 1947, they unveiled the first commercial microwave oven, the *Radarange.* But this wasn't your countertop convenience: it stood nearly 6 feet tall, weighed around 750 pounds, and cost a whopping $5,000 (equivalent to about $65,000 today). It was mainly used in restaurants and ships, not exactly something you could use to reheat coffee in your pajamas.

It took a couple of decades, but by the 1960s and '70s, engineers had shrunk the technology to something far more manageable and affordable. At first, consumers were wary. The idea of "radiation in the kitchen" spooked people. Companies had to run ad campaigns assuring the public that, no, your microwave wouldn't fry your brain or make your food glow in the dark.

Eventually, convenience won the day. You could defrost a steak, heat soup, or pop popcorn in minutes. The microwave oven became the unsung hero of late-night leftovers, dorm room meals, and busy parents everywhere. Today, over 90% of U.S. households have one humming in their kitchens. All thanks to a melted candy bar and a curious engineer who paid attention to his snack.

Fascinating Facts

- It Was Never Meant for Food: Percy Spencer's microwave breakthrough came by accident. He was testing radar, not trying to cook lunch.
- The First Models Were Monsters: The original Radarange stood nearly as tall as a refrigerator, required plumbing for water cooling, and cost more than a car.
- Microwave Myths Persist: Despite decades of safe use, myths about microwave radiation linger. Yet the appliance does not make food radioactive; it just makes it hot!

To Learn More

- Ponti, Crystal. "Who Invented the Microwave Oven?" *History.com*, April 28, 2025. This article explores how engineer Percy Spencer accidentally discovered microwave cooking while working on radar technology, sparking a kitchen revolution. https://tinyurl.com/microwave-invention
- History of ideas. "The Accidental Invention That Changed Kitchens Forever: The Microwave!"

YouTube, Nov 5, 2024. This video tells the surprising story of how a melting chocolate bar led to the invention of the microwave oven, transforming how we cook forever. https://tinyurl.com/microwave-invention-video

PENICILLIN: THE MOLDY MISTAKE THAT SAVES MILLIONS

If you've ever taken antibiotics for strep throat, an infected cut, or a sinus infection, you owe a big thanks to a forgetful scientist and a fuzzy blob of mold.

It was a case of "oops" that turned into "Eureka!" It was 1928. Scottish bacteriologist Alexander Fleming had just returned from vacation to his famously messy lab at St. Mary's Hospital in London. While tidying up, he noticed that one of his Petri dishes of staphylococcus bacteria had been contaminated by a fuzzy mold. But here's the weird part: the area around the mold was completely clear of bacteria. Most people would've said *"ew,"* and tossed it in the trash. Fleming, however, leaned in.

The mold, he discovered, was *Penicillium notatum*, and it was producing a substance that killed bacteria without harming human cells. Fleming had stumbled onto the world's first natural antibiotic entirely by accident. He named the miracle substance penicillin.

Now, here's where it gets sticky (not unlike mold). Fleming was a brilliant observer but not a great developer. While he proved penicillin's ability to kill bacteria in the lab, he couldn't find a way to purify or mass-produce it. So, for a while, this life-saving medicine sat in obscurity, growing mold in both petri dishes and public interest.

Fast forward to the early 1940s, as World War II raged and infections were taking more lives than bullets. Enter a trio of scientific heroes: Howard Florey, Ernst Chain, and Norman Heatley from Oxford University. They revived Fleming's forgotten discovery and figured out how to extract and produce penicillin in usable form. But even then, yields were low.

So, where did the breakthrough come from? *A rotting cantaloupe* in a Peoria, Illinois grocery store. Seriously. The mold on this humble melon turned out to be a penicillin-producing machine.

Thanks to American scientists, fermentation tanks, and a little produce-section luck, penicillin was rolled out just in time to treat thousands of Allied troops suffering from infected wounds. By the end of World War II, penicillin was hailed as a "wonder drug," and with good reason. It had saved countless lives and would go on to save millions more in the decades to come.

Today, penicillin is still widely used to treat everything from ear infections to syphilis. It kicked off the antibiotic era and made once-deadly infections a nuisance at worst. It all started with a messy lab, an observant scientist, a lucky accident, and one moldy plate of science magic.

Fascinating Facts

- A Discovery Almost Trashed: Fleming nearly threw out the moldy dish, but noticed the bacteria-free zone just in time. That little ring of clarity would become the starting point of modern antibiotics.
- The Cantaloupe That Saved the World: Scientists in Illinois screened thousands of moldy fruits before stumbling on a cantaloupe strain that produced 600 times more penicillin than Fleming's.
- From Forgotten to Nobel-Worthy: Fleming, Florey, and Chain shared the 1945 Nobel Prize in Medicine, proving that sometimes, science takes a team, and a fungus.

To Learn More

- ACS Chemistry for Life. "Discovery and Development of Penicillin." This article details how Alexander Fleming's accidental discovery of penicillin in 1928 sparked a medical breakthrough that revolutionized the treatment of bacterial infections. https://tinyurl.com/discovery-of-penicillin
- PBS. "The Discovery of Penicillin." *PBS Learning Media*, December 25, 2015. This educational video explains how the discovery of penicillin marked the beginning of the antibiotic era, saving millions of lives and revolutionizing modern medicine. https://tinyurl.com/discovery-of-penicillin-video

THE STICKY INSPIRATION FROM NATURE

It all started with a Swiss dog walk and a really annoying burr.

In 1941, engineer George de Mestral went for a hike in the Alps with his trusty dog. When he returned home, he noticed his pants and the dog's fur were absolutely covered in those pesky burrs that cling like they've got a grudge. Instead of just picking them off and moving on, de Mestral did what any great inventor would do. He got curious. Under a microscope, he found the secret. Each burr was covered in tiny hooks that latched onto anything looped or fuzzy. Nature, it seemed, had invented its own fastening system.

Inspired by this sticky situation, de Mestral set out to mimic the burr's structure. After years of experimenting with fabric and industrial weaving techniques, he created a two-part fastener: one side with tiny hooks, the other with soft loops. Snap them together, and voilà! They held tight, then peeled apart with a satisfying rip. He named it Velcro, a mash-up of the French words "velours" (meaning 'velvet') and "crochet" (meaning 'hook').

But not everyone saw the brilliance at first. Manufacturers thought it was a gimmick. Fashion designers turned up their noses at the synthetic material. It wasn't until NASA adopted Velcro for securing tools and gear in zero gravity during the Apollo missions that the world took notice. If it was good enough for astronauts, surely it was good enough for the rest of us!

From that point on, Velcro's popularity skyrocketed. It showed up in sneakers, ski jackets, blood pressure cuffs, and baby diapers. Firefighters rely on it to quickly suit up. Paramedics use it to secure equipment. Even the U.S. military integrated it into their gear. And now? Engineers are experimenting with miniature versions for soft robotics and surgical tools. Velcro has gone from a fuzzy forest nuisance to a staple of modern convenience.

Not bad for a guy who paid attention to what was stuck to his dog.

Fascinating Facts

- Nature's Influence: Velcro's design mimics the tiny hooks found on burdock burrs, turning an annoyance into an innovation.
- NASA Approved: Velcro became a crucial part of astronaut suits and equipment, helping keep objects secure in zero gravity.
- Velcro Name Origins: The name comes from a blend of "velours" (French for velvet) and "crochet" (hook)—describing its loop-and-hook fastening system.

To Learn More

- Cosi's Science Now. "How Did Nature's Design Lead to Velcro's Creation? | COSI's Science Now with Dr. Marci Howdyshell." *YouTube*, March 19, 2020. This well-done video explains how Swiss engineer George de Mestral was inspired by burrs clinging to his dog's fur—leading to the invention of Velcro

through biomimicry. https://tinyurl.com/velcro-creation-video
- Velcro Companies. "An Idea that Stuck: How George de Mestral Invented the Velcro Brand Fastener." *Velcro.com blog*, November 11, 2016. This blog post tells the origin story of Velcro, from a curious nature walk to the creation of one of the world's most widely used fasteners. https://tinyurl.com/velcro-creation

THE POST-IT NOTE: AN ACCIDENTAL INVENTION

Post-it Notes, those colorful little squares that fill offices, notebooks, and brainstorming sessions worldwide, were never supposed to exist!

In 1968, Spencer Silver, a chemist at 3M, was attempting to develop a super-strong adhesive, one that could be used in aircraft construction. But, *oops*, what he ended up with was the opposite. Instead of a glue that gripped like a gorilla, he created one that barely stuck at all. It didn't bond materials permanently, but it also didn't fall off. It could be reused. And reused again.

Most researchers might have scrapped it and moved on. But Silver knew he'd stumbled on something interesting. He just didn't know what for. For years, he struggled to find a purpose for his invention.

Enter Art Fry, a fellow 3M employee with a choir-boy problem. In 1974, Fry was singing in his church choir and getting increasingly annoyed that his paper bookmarks kept slipping out of his hymnal. Then he remembered Silver's weird, low-tack glue. Could it hold a piece of paper in place without damaging the page? Fry coated some paper with Silver's adhesive and voilà. The first sticky note didn't fall off and didn't leave a mark. Perfect for hymns. Perfect for everything. And just like that, the Post-It Note was born.

However, the story didn't end with invention; it also needed a revolution in marketing. Convincing people of this invention's genius wasn't a walk in the park. When 3M first introduced them under the name "Press 'n Peel," people were confused. Why would anyone need this oddly clingy paper?

It wasn't until 1978, during a test market campaign dubbed the "Boise Blitz" in Boise, Idaho, that the Post-it Note finally took hold, both literally and figuratively. Free samples were handed out to local businesses, and the response was overwhelmingly positive: 90% of users said they'd buy them again. Just like that, a new office essential was born.

Today, Post-it Notes are everywhere, from classrooms and boardrooms to brainstorming sessions and household to-do lists. They come in all shapes, colors, and sizes. Artists create murals with them. Students plot essays with them. Office workers slap them on every visible surface. They've even gone digital, with virtual sticky note apps mimicking their analog charm. Not bad for a failed glue.

And here's the best part: without one man's failed adhesive and another man's hymn-book headache, the world might never have known the joy of peeling off that little yellow square and feeling like your entire life is, finally, organized.

Fascinating Facts

- Invented Backward: Spencer Silver accidentally discovered the glue while trying to make something stronger. Instead, he got a weak, removable, reusable adhesive that could stick to surfaces without leaving residue.
- Yellow Was a Fluke: The original yellow color wasn't strategic—it just happened to be the scrap paper color available next to the lab. It stuck!
- They Took Years to Catch On: Despite the invention being ready in the mid-70s, Post-it Notes didn't launch nationally until 1980, once 3M realized people had to *use* them to *want* them.

To Learn More

- Post-It.com: History Timeline: Post-It notes. This official timeline traces the accidental invention and global success of Post-It Notes, born from a failed attempt to create a super-strong adhesive. https://tinyurl.com/post-it-timeline
- NBC News Learn. "Chance Discoveries: Post-It Notes." *YouTube,* May 2, 2020. This video explores how an unsticky glue and a bookmark problem led to one of the most iconic office supplies in history, thanks to creative thinking and a bit of luck. https://tinyurl.com/post-it-discovery-video

CRISPY REVENGE: THE ORIGIN OF THE POTATO CHIP

It started with a huffy diner and a salty comeback and ended with the creation of one of the world's most addictive snacks.

The year was 1853, and the place was Moon's Lake House, a swanky resort restaurant in Saratoga Springs, New York. George Crum, a talented cook of Native American and African American descent, was known for his sharp skills, a sharp personality, and a stubborn streak. He was working in the kitchen when a picky customer sent back his fried potatoes several times, complaining they were too thick, soggy, and just not good enough. Crum, understandably annoyed and not one to take criticism lightly, decided to give the man exactly what he *didn't* ask for. He sliced the potatoes paper-thin, fried them until extra crispy, and doused them in salt. They were so salty they practically crunched back.

It was meant to be a joke. A salty, crunchy *"that'll show him"* dish.

But the customer loved them. The result? An accidental masterpiece. While legend often credits railroad magnate Cornelius Vanderbilt as the picky customer behind this happy accident, there's no definitive evidence linking him to the story. Still, it makes for a great bit of salty folklore.

Word spread quickly, and that kitchen prank became an instant hit. Diners at Moon's started requesting the crispy, salty treats by name. They became known as "Saratoga Chips." Crum soon opened his own restaurant, where every table got a complimentary basket. The chips were made fresh, served warm, and quickly became the most talked-about side dish in New York.

Saratoga Chips stayed a regional delicacy until the 1920s when the snack went commercial. As mass production and packaging became possible, companies realized that chips weren't just a restaurant snack; they could be sold by the bag. Then came the flavor boom: barbecue in the 1950s, sour cream and onion in the '60s, and an explosion of chip creativity ever since.

Today, potato chips are close to a $40 billion global industry and an icon of snack culture. Americans alone munch their way through over 1.5 billion pounds of chips annually. All this thanks to complaint, a clever cook, and a very dramatic act of passive-aggressive frying.

Fascinating Facts

- Born Out of Spite: The first potato chips were reportedly made to annoy a customer, but instead launched a global snack sensation.
- The Crum Legacy: George Crum's restaurant became a hotspot for Saratoga socialites. Though some credit also goes to his sister, Kate Wicks, and even several others, Crum's name is forever linked to the birth of the chip.
- Billions Served, Billions Made: Today, potato chips are consumed in over 100 countries and comprise a significant portion of the global snack food market.

The average American eats over 4 pounds of chips per year.

To Learn More

- Daugherty, Greg. "Who Invented the Potato Chip? It's Complicated." *History Channel,* February 03, 2021. This article explores the debated origins of the potato chip, tracing its salty beginnings to a legendary 1853 culinary clash in Saratoga Springs. https://tinyurl.com/who-invented-the-potato-chip
- Daily Dose Documentary. "History of Potato Chips: Who Invented the Potato Chip?" *YouTube,* Jun 13, 2023. This video breaks down the crunchy controversy behind who really invented the potato chip, blending food history with a dash of folklore. https://tinyurl.com/history-of-potato-chip-video

THE UNEXPECTED ORIGINS OF THE TOOTHBRUSH

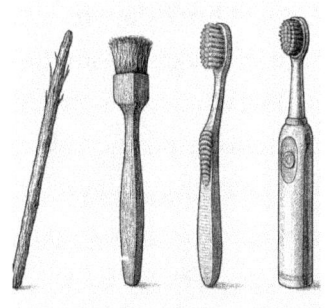

We brush, we rinse, we repeat, twice a day, every day. But have you ever stopped mid-scrub to wonder how your trusty toothbrush came to be? This daily ritual hides a wild, centuries-long saga involving ancient chew sticks, Siberian pigs, a jailed British riot starter, and a toothbrush that started in a prison cell.

Imagine a world where brushing your teeth meant chewing on a stick. Sounds odd, right? But that's exactly how our ancient ancestors tackled dental hygiene. The Babylonians, for instance, were pioneers in this. They used frayed twigs known as "chewing sticks" to clean away the remnants of their ancient feasts. These primitive brushes worked like a natural floss-and-scrub combo. Similar methods were found in Egypt, China, India, and Africa. Ancient Egyptians even took them to the grave, literally. Archaeologists have found them tucked inside tombs, proving that good dental hygiene was considered worthy of the afterlife.

Now, jump to the Tang Dynasty in China, around 600 AD, where someone had the bright idea to attach bristles to a handle, creating a tool that might have started to resemble the toothbrush we know today. These brushes used bamboo or bone handles and boar bristles from the necks of Siberian pigs. The bristles were stiff, wiry, and durable (though not exactly gentle on the gums). This "pig brush" innovation eventually made its way to Europe, although it took the Western world a while to catch on.

Then came William Addis, an 18th-century Englishman. The legend goes that Addis was thrown into Newgate Prison for inciting a riot. While behind bars, he watched a guard sweeping the floor and had a moment of inspiration. If a broom could clean dirty floors, why not use something similar to clean teeth? He drilled holes into a small bone, shoved in some bristles, and voilà, one jailhouse toothbrush. Genius move! Once out of jail, Addis turned his makeshift creation into a booming business, producing the first mass-marketed toothbrushes in England. His company, which eventually morphed into Wisdom Toothbrushes, became a household name. The business stayed within the family until 1996. Addis is often referred to as the "Father of Modern Oral Hygiene."

But it was the 20th century that gave the toothbrush its glow-up. In 1938, DuPont introduced nylon bristles, finally ending our long, uncomfortable relationship with hog hair. Suddenly, toothbrushes were more hygienic and comfortable. This sparked a toothbrush revolution. By the 1960s, electric toothbrushes hit the market, promising better plaque removal and serious dental hygiene. Today, our toothbrushes come with Bluetooth, timers, pressure sensors, and AI-powered apps. Some even connect to your phone to give you a brushing report card because, apparently, your molars need metrics now.

And what's brushing without the paste? Before sleek tubes and minty gels, the story of toothpaste was a gritty tale of trial and error (emphasis on the grit.) Ancient Egyptians, as far back as 5000 BCE, created one of the first known dental pastes by mixing crushed ox hooves, ashes, burnt eggshells, and pumice. Effective? Probably. Pleasant? Not so much. But it gets better (or worse): the Greeks and Romans upped the abrasiveness by adding crushed bones and oyster shells, sometimes with a dash of charcoal or bark for good measure.

Meanwhile, in ancient China and India, toothpaste formulas focused more on breath-freshening and medicinal herbs. The Chinese mixed ginseng, salt, and herbal mints, which proved to be decidedly more refreshing.

Toothpaste as we know it didn't emerge until the 1800s. Early modern versions included soap (yes, actual soap) and chalk. By the 1890s, inspired by artists' paint containers, toothpaste finally made its way into collapsible tubes. It wasn't until the 1950s that fluoride was introduced, marking a true turning point in cavity prevention and dental health. Today's toothpaste boasts a cocktail of ingredients: fluoride for strengthening enamel, abrasives for polishing, detergents for foaming, and flavoring agents.

So, the next time you reach for that high-tech electric brush or squeeze out a dab of minty gel, take a moment to thank the prisoners, the pigs, and the ancient inventors who paved the way.

Fascinating Facts

- Toothbrushes Got a U.S. Debut in 1885: That's when the first mass-produced toothbrush hit the American market. However, brushing didn't become a common habit in the U.S. until after World War II, when soldiers returned home with strict hygiene routines.
- Nylon Changed Everything in 1938: DuPont's invention of nylon made toothbrushes cleaner, longer-lasting, and much less swine-based. Goodbye, boar bristles; hello, smooth brushing.
- Electric Brushes Energized the Market: First introduced in the 1950s, electric toothbrushes were initially designed for people with limited dexterity. Now, they're a standard in dental care.

To Learn More

- Avishkaar Nexus. "Who Invented the Toothbrush? A 5000-Year Tale of Clean Teeth." *YouTube*, Nov 28, 2024. This video traces the fascinating 5,000-year

journey of the toothbrush, from ancient chew sticks to modern dental care tools. https://tinyurl.com/invention-of-toothbrush-video
- Warner, Deborah. "A brush with history." *Smithsonian, National Museum of American History*, October 31, 2022. This Smithsonian article examines the evolution of toothbrushes in America, including quirky innovations and the rise of mass-produced oral hygiene products. https://tinyurl.com/toothbrush-history
- The History Guy. "Toothpaste: A History of Oral Hygiene." *YouTube*. May 22, 2023. This video explores the surprisingly rich history of toothpaste, from its origins in crushed shells and charcoal to modern minty gels and tubes. https://tinyurl.com/toothpaste-history-video

CORN FLAKES: BREAKFAST'S MOST ACCIDENTAL ICON

It might be hard to imagine a world without cereal boxes crowding the breakfast aisle, but one of the most famous morning meals, Corn Flakes, was never supposed to happen in the first place. Like so many quirky inventions, it was born out of a mistake.

The story begins in 1894 at the Battle Creek Sanitarium in Michigan, where Dr. John Harvey Kellogg, a strict health reformer, and his brother, Will Keith Kellogg, were developing bland, vegetarian foods for their patients. This place wasn't just about healing the body; it was about purifying the soul. Dr. Kellogg was convinced that bland, meatless food could help. Why? Because he believed rich, flavorful meals led to sinful thoughts and self-indulgence. And by "self-indulgence," he mostly meant *you know what*.

Enter his brother, Will Keith Kellogg, who worked alongside him at the Sanitarium. Together, they experimented with different vegetarian foods, hoping to create something nutritious, easy to digest, and so bland it wouldn't tempt even the lustiest of souls. One day in 1894, while cooking up a batch of wheat-based dough for bread, the brothers got distracted and accidentally left the boiled wheat sitting out too long. Instead of a soggy mess, they came back to find it dried and stale. Being resourceful (and frugal), they ran it through rollers to flatten it, and out popped thin flakes. Curious, they tried the same process with corn instead of wheat. A quick bake later, the world's first dry breakfast cereal was born. It was crunchy. It was strange. It was bland. But it was weirdly delightful. They began serving it to the patients at the Sanitarium.

Dr. Kellogg, naturally, wanted to keep it pure and sugar-free. But Will saw more than a health food. He saw *breakfast gold*. He wanted to add sugar to make the flakes more palatable to the masses. John Harvey flat-out refused, insisting the product remain piously plain. So, Will went rogue, snuck in some sugar, and launched his own company. In 1906, he founded the Battle Creek Toasted Corn Flake Company, later known as Kellogg's, and began producing a sweeter version of the cereal. People loved it. The sugary version became a massive hit with the public, and cornflakes quickly found their way into breakfast bowls around the globe.

Thus, the tale of one of the greatest sibling rivalries in culinary history: one brother fighting to save souls through bland breakfasts, the other launching a billion-dollar empire one spoonful of sugar at a time.

And the best part? All of it, the flakes, the feud, the fortune, started with a forgotten pot of wheat dough.

Fascinating Facts

- An Oops-Turned-Empire: A single pot of overcooked grain launched what would become a multibillion-dollar cereal industry, and the birth of the iconic Kellogg's brand.
- Cereal with a Side of Morals: Dr. John Kellogg's original cornflakes were intentionally bland, based on his belief that flavorful foods encouraged sinful behavior.
- Sugar vs. Sanctity: The Kellogg brothers parted ways over the decision to add sugar to cornflakes. Will's sweetened version became a commercial hit; John was not amused.

To Learn More

- Pruitt, Sarah. "Cereal: The Accidental Invention That Changed American Breakfast." *History.com*. This article tells how a culinary accident at a health sanitarium led to the creation of cornflakes and

sparked a breakfast revolution across America. https://tinyurl.com/cereal-breakfast-origins
- History of Food. "Kellogg's: The Breakfast Revolution!" *YouTube*, Feb 19, 2025. This well-done video explores how the Kellogg brothers turned a bland health food experiment into a global breakfast empire. https://tinyurl.com/breakfast-revolution-video

6

BIZARRE COINCIDENCES & SYNCHRONICITIES

Some stories make you laugh. Others make you think. And then there are those that make you pause, raise an eyebrow, and mutter, *"Okay, that's just weird."* This chapter is full of those moments. Real-life tales so bizarrely timed, so eerily connected, you'd swear the universe was pulling a fast one. From long-lost twins living eerily parallel lives to fictional tales that somehow predicted real disasters to Founding Fathers who couldn't stop dying on the Fourth of July, these strange-but-true events are pure dinner party gold. Are they fate? Fluke? Or is the cosmos just showing off? Whatever the cause, these stories prove that sometimes, the universe really does have a punchline.

THE TWIN BROTHERS WITH IDENTICAL LIVES

When it comes to weird coincidences, this one reads like a script for a psychological thriller. Imagine discovering that someone else has been living your life down to the smallest detail.

Meet Jim Lewis and Jim Springer, identical twin brothers separated at birth. They were adopted into different families and unaware of each other's existence for nearly four decades. But when they finally met in 1979, what they discovered wasn't just a family connection. It was a mirror.

It began in 1940. Twin boys were separated when they were just weeks old in Ohio and adopted by different families. Unbeknownst to each other, their adoptive parents decided on the name "James" for each of them.

As they grew up, Jim Lewis and Jim Springer (still unaware of each other) lived remarkably parallel lives. Both named their dogs "Toy." Both married women named Linda and then divorced them. Then, they each remarried to women named Betty. And if you're thinking this can't get any stranger, each Jim named his son James Allen (with one spelling it "Alan" and the other "Allen"). Their shared interests didn't end with family life. They both enjoyed woodworking, smoked Salem cigarettes, drank Miller Lite, and drove light-blue Chevrolets. Both worked in law enforcement as deputy sheriffs. Even their choice of vacation spots was identical, with both heading to the same beach in Florida. It's as if they were living parallel lives, each echoing the other's choices.

And they didn't even know the other existed.

When they finally met at age 39, thanks to a search through adoption records, they were understandably shocked. So were the researchers at the University of Minnesota's twin studies program, who quickly brought the two Jims in for testing. Their brain waves, heart rates, and personality traits were freakishly alike. It was like someone had duplicated a life with uncanny precision. The scientists were unable to fully explain it.

The Jim Twins' story remains one of the most famous and baffling examples of synchronicity ever recorded. Genetics might explain some of it. But the matching wives, dogs, cars, beer brands, and vacation spots? That veers into *"universe-is-playing-a-prank"* territory.

The twins' lives fuel the debate on nature versus nurture, suggesting that while the environment plays a role, genetics might have a stronger hand in the matter. Their story makes us wonder: How much of who we are is written in our DNA, and how much is shaped by the world around us? It's a question that continues to mystify scientists and philosophers alike, leaving us pondering the mysterious interplay between our genetic blueprints and the lives we lead.

Whatever the cause, their story has become the gold standard in real-life synchronicity—so improbable, so precise, it sounds scripted. But every word of it is true.

Fascinating Facts

- Separated at Birth: The twins were adopted into different families and raised just 40 miles apart—neither knowing the other existed for nearly four decades.
- Name Game: Both were named James, had sons named James, married women named Linda, then Betty, and owned dogs named Toy.
- Science Scratched Its Head: After their reunion, the Jim Twins were studied by psychologists and twin researchers. Their biometric similarities and life parallels were *far beyond statistical norms.*

To Learn More

- Chen, Edwin. "Twins Reared Apart: A Living Lab." *The New York Times,* December 9, 1979. This New York Times article explores the groundbreaking case of twins separated at birth who grew up with astonishing similarities, fueling debates about nature versus nurture. https://tinyurl.com/twins-reared-apart
- HaveSomeFun 3344. "Johnny Carson Memories: The Jim Twins." *YouTube*, December 1, 2022. This fascinating video revisits the famous Tonight Show segment featuring Johnny Carson's interview with the "Jim Twins." https://tinyurl.com/carson-twins-interview

THE EERIE COINCIDENCES OF THE TITANIC AND THE TITAN

If you pitch this to a movie studio, they may laugh you out of the room for being too far-fetched. But truth, as it often does, proves stranger than fiction.

Back in 1898, a full 14 years before the Titanic's maiden voyage, an American author named Morgan Robertson wrote a novella titled *Futility, or the Wreck of the Titan*. The story followed a massive, luxurious ocean liner called the Titan, the largest vessel of its kind ever built. Unsinkable, they said. Spoiler alert: It sank.

Sound familiar? *Wait*, it gets weirder.

In the novella, the Titan sails across the North Atlantic in April. During its journey, it strikes an iceberg and sinks to the bottom of the sea. There aren't enough lifeboats for passengers. Many lives are lost. The ship's specifications (length, tonnage, speed) are eerily close to those of the real-life RMS Titanic, whose 1912 voyage mirrored Robertson's narrative in unsettling ways. With dimensions that bore a striking resemblance to those of the Titan, the "unsinkable" Titanic was a marvel of its time. However, despite its grandeur, the Titanic's tragic end echoed the fictional ship's story, with many lives lost due to the insufficient number of lifeboats. The iceberg that sealed its fate loomed large in the dark waters of the North Atlantic, much like the one that brought down the Titan. Same size, same fate, same icy grave.

The comparisons between the fictional Titan and the doomed Titanic are so jaw-droppingly similar that people have speculated for decades: Did Robertson have a vision? A premonition? Access to a time machine?

Not quite. When questioned about the striking parallels, Robertson explained he had drawn on his maritime experience and trends in shipbuilding. He was a seasoned seafarer who kept up with naval engineering and knew that ships were being built larger and faster with little regard for safety. His story, he claimed, was an extrapolation of what could go wrong. Turns out, he was right, right down to the icy details.

Still, the coincidences are enough to send a shiver down your spine. Titan and Titanic were practically twins in tragedy:

- Both had similar names.
- Both were British passenger liners.
- Both were described as unsinkable.
- Both collided with an iceberg in the North Atlantic in April.
- Both were around 800 feet long.
- Both carried around 3,000 people and lost more than half.
- Both had woefully inadequate lifeboats.

While most historians chalk it up to a chilling example of informed imagination, others still marvel at how close fiction came to mirroring reality.

Whatever the explanation, Futility is one of the most astonishing literary coincidences in modern history. It has become a cult curiosity among literary and historical circles. This cautionary tale was strangely ahead of its time. Whether it's seen as prophecy or just one giant cosmic coincidence, the story of the Titan reminds us that sometimes life doesn't just imitate art; it steals the script and drowns with it.

Fascinating Facts

- "Titan" vs. Titanic: Robertson's fictional *Titan* was only 25 meters shorter than the real Titanic. Both were labeled "unsinkable."
- Same Month, Same Cause: Both ships hit an iceberg and sank in April in the North Atlantic while traveling at similar speeds and facing lifeboat shortages.
- Fiction Becomes Fact: After the Titanic disaster, *Futility* was republished with the subtitle "The Wreck of the Titan" and quickly became a global sensation.

To Learn More

- Shaw, Gabbi. "A novella published 14 years before the Titanic sank seemed to have predicted the disaster." *Business Insider,* June 28, 2023. This article explores the uncanny parallels between the 1898 novella *Futility,* later retitled *The Wreck of the Titan* and the real-life sinking of the Titanic. https://tinyurl.com/novella-predicts-the-titanic
- Tiger Media Network. "Wreck Of The Titan: A foretelling of disaster or interesting coincidence."

YouTube, April 19, 2024. This well-done video examines whether *The Wreck of the Titan* was a chilling prophecy or just a remarkable coincidence foreshadowing the Titanic tragedy. https://tinyurl.com/titanic-foretelling-video

LINCOLN AND KENNEDY: PARALLELS BEYOND BELIEF

Let's dive into the uncanny similarities between two of America's most iconic presidents, Abraham Lincoln and John F. Kennedy.

Both were elected to Congress in years ending in '46—Lincoln in 1846 and Kennedy in 1946. Fast forward to their presidential elections, and you'll find another eerie match: Lincoln was elected in 1860, while Kennedy took office exactly a century later, in 1960. Both had presidential campaigns with famous debates: the Lincoln/Douglas debates and the Kennedy/Nixon debates. Both lost a son while living in the White House. Both were notably concerned with civil rights. Lincoln issued the Emancipation Proclamation; Kennedy proposed the Civil Rights Act of 1964.

When it comes to their vice presidents, the coincidences don't stop. Lincoln had Andrew Johnson, and Kennedy had Lyndon Johnson. Both men named Johnson stepped up as President following the tragic assassinations of their predecessors.

And speaking of assassinations, both Lincoln and Kennedy were shot in the head on a Friday while sitting next to their wives. Lincoln was shot at Ford's Theatre; Kennedy was shot in a Lincoln car made by Ford. Their assassins? John Wilkes Booth and Lee Harvey Oswald, both known by three-part names, added yet another layer to this web of connections. Both Booth and Oswald were killed before their trials and within the same month as the assassination.

These parallels have sparked countless discussions and theories over the years. Some folks have jumped to conclusions, claiming supernatural forces or divine intervention. However, a closer examination of historical records sheds light on the origins and accuracy of these claims. Many parallels turn out to be cherry-picked or exaggerated, while others fall apart under scrutiny. For instance, the idea that Lincoln had a secretary named Kennedy and vice versa is a pure myth. Yet, despite the inaccuracies, these coincidences continue to capture the public's imagination, feeding into conspiracy theories and popular culture. When we see Lincoln and Kennedy's lives aligning in such peculiar ways, we can't help but wonder if there's more to the story. Our brains are wired to search for order, and these parallels provide a perfect playground for our imaginations to run wild. They add a layer of intrigue to the legacies of these presidents, transforming simple historical facts into tantalizing stories that linger in our consciousness.

The impact of these coincidences extends beyond mere trivia; they've shaped cultural and historical narratives in fascinating ways. Conspiracy theorists have woven elaborate tales, suggesting everything from time travel to secret societies manipulating the world's affairs. Meanwhile, in pop culture, these parallels have inspired countless books, films, and TV shows that explore the mysteries of fate and destiny. The idea of two great leaders, separated by a century yet connected by a web of coincidences, is a story too captivating to ignore. It's a narrative that blurs the line between history and mythology, inviting us to ponder the forces that shape our world.

Fascinating Facts

- Elections: Lincoln was elected to Congress in 1846 and Kennedy in 1946. Lincoln was elected President in 1860, and Kennedy in 1960.
- Assassination Days: Both were assassinated on a Friday, shot in the head, and in the presence of their wives.
- Location: Lincoln was shot in Ford's Theatre. Kennedy was shot in a Ford car, specifically, a Lincoln Continental, while passing through Dallas's Dealey Plaza (formerly a theater district).
- Successors: Each was succeeded by his Vice President, who was named Johnson.
- Assassins' Fate: Both assassins were killed before their trials could be held.

To Learn More

- Mikkelson, David. "Are These 'Coincidences' Linking Lincoln to Kennedy Real?" *Snopes Fact Check*, June 11, 1999. This fact-checking article separates truth from myth in the widely circulated list of eerie similarities between Presidents Lincoln and

Kennedy. https://tinyurl.com/lincoln-kennedy-fact-check
- Mr. Beat. "All Those Weird Lincoln Kennedy Coincidences." *YouTube,* April 9, 2021. This video delves into the strange parallels often drawn between Lincoln and Kennedy, exploring which are factual and which are just fun folklore. https://tinyurl.com/lincoln-kennedy-video
- Book recommendation: Knight, Jonathan. "The Lincoln-Kennedy Coincidences: Fact and Legend in the Assassinations." *Exposit Books*, January 6, 2023. This book examines the famous Lincoln-Kennedy coincidences through a historical lens, distinguishing between remarkable facts and exaggerated legends.

SIR ANTHONY HOPKINS: WHEN THE UNIVERSE CASTS THE RIGHT ACTOR

Sometimes, the universe doesn't just cast the right actor; it practically throws the script at them.

In the late 1970s, legendary actor Sir Anthony Hopkins was preparing for a lead role in the film adaptation of *The Girl from Petrovka,* a Cold War-era romance written by American journalist and author George Feifer. Hopkins, known for immersing himself in roles with the dedication of a master craftsman, wanted to read the novel to gain a deeper understanding of his character. There was just one problem: the book was out of print.

No worries, he thought. Surely, one of London's many bookstores would have a dusty copy on some forgotten shelf. So, Hopkins went hunting. Shop after shop, shelf after shelf. Nothing. The book was nowhere to be found.

Frustrated and about to give up, Hopkins walked into the London Underground. As he waited on the platform, he glanced at the bench beside him. There, as if placed by divine appointment, was a lone book. Curious, he picked it up.

The Girl from Petrovka.

Not just any edition; it was heavily annotated. It was full of notes scribbled in the margins, highlighted passages, underlines, and edits. Someone had really *lived* in this book.

Fast forward a few weeks. Hopkins, now on set, met George Feifer. In passing, Hopkins told him the bizarre story of how he had found the book. Feifer blinked. *"Wait... did it have notes in the margins?"* Hopkins nodded. Feifer's jaw dropped.

Feifer explained that he had lost his *personal* annotated copy of the manuscript in London years earlier. He'd been devastated, unable to find it again. And here it was. Somehow, Hopkins had picked up that very edition, by total accident, in a random subway station. It was returned to him not by a courier or lost-and-found clerk but by the man chosen to play the film's lead.

In a city of millions, with thousands of benches, in a moment that can only be described as cinematic fate, Hopkins had found *the exact copy* Feifer had lost.

Coincidence? Cosmic casting call? Divine prank? Whatever you call it, it's a real-life plot twist worthy of its own film.

Fascinating Facts

- The Impossible Find: Hopkins was looking for *any* copy of the novel. The one he found happened to be the author's own marked-up copy, which had been lost weeks earlier.
- The Author Was Stunned: When George Feifer saw the book in Hopkins' hands, he immediately identified it as his personal manuscript, complete with notes he'd written during the book's creation.
- A Rare Case of Real-Life Synchronicity: This event remains one of the most widely cited documented coincidences involving an actor, an author, and a missing book with a very strange travel history.

To Learn More:

- Dison, Brad. "The Lost Book." *Natchitoches Parish Journal*, May 11, 2022. This article recounts the unbelievable true story of how actor Anthony Hopkins stumbled upon a long-lost book that played a pivotal role in his career—thanks to an extraordinary coincidence. https://tinyurl.com/hopkins-and-the-lost-book
- Taylor, Tom. "How Anthony Hopkins became the centre of the quantum theory of coincidence. *Far Out*, April 21, 2023. This piece explores how a bizarre literary twist in Anthony Hopkins' life became a case study in synchronicity and the strange

science of chance encounters. https://tinyurl.com/hopkins-and-coincidence

HISTORY'S PERFECT TIMING: THE DAY JEFFERSON AND ADAMS DIED

Some historical coincidences are so poetic, so perfectly timed, they feel like the work of a divine screenwriter. Case in point: the death of two of America's most influential Founding Fathers, Thomas Jefferson and John Adams. On July 4, 1826, exactly 50 years to the day after the Declaration of Independence was adopted, both men drew their final breaths. It's the kind of history nugget that sounds too coincidental to be true, yet it really happened.

Jefferson and Adams weren't just statesmen; they were a two-man political drama. They were once close collaborators in the revolution, co-architects of independence, and co-signers of the Declaration itself. But over time, their friendship fractured into political rivalry. Jefferson (a Democratic-Republican) and Adams (a Federalist) clashed on nearly every issue, from the scope of government power to foreign policy.

And yet, in their golden years, something remarkable happened. They reconciled, not through dramatic speeches or stage-worthy reunions, but through good old-fashioned letter-writing. Over the course of 14 years, the two exchanged over 150 letters, delving deeply into philosophy, democracy, and even mortality. They became pen pals with purpose, writing not just as former foes but as men trying to make sense of the legacy they were leaving behind.

Then came that legendary July 4.

Adams, then 90 years old and living in Massachusetts, lay on his deathbed. His last words, according to lore, were: "Thomas Jefferson still survives." The twist? Jefferson had passed away just a few hours earlier at Monticello, Virginia, at the age of 83.

Neither knew the other's exact fate in those final moments. It was as if the universe conspired to bring their intertwined stories to a simultaneous, symbolic close. For a nation still finding its feet, the double loss on Independence Day was as eerie as it was inspiring. Daniel Webster's eulogy for Adams and Jefferson spoke to a point that many people believed: that something other than coincidence was at work.

Coincidence? Divine timing? A narrative flourish written by the cosmos itself?

And if that wasn't enough to make the hair on your arms stand up, James Monroe, the fifth U.S. President and another Founding Father died on—you guessed it—July 4, 1831. That's *three* of America's first five presidents dying on the same symbolic day. Coincidence? Fate? Patriotism taken to a metaphysical extreme? Whatever you believe, it's a story that's earned its place in every history book and trivia night worth attending.

Fascinating Facts

- The Olive Branch: Once allies, then fierce political opponents, their famous reconciliation began on January 1, 1812, when John Adams wrote a brief yet poignant note to Jefferson. Jefferson replied warningly. Over the next 14 years, they exchanged 158 letters.
- 50 Years to the Day: Both men died on July 4, 1826, exactly 50 years after the Declaration of Independence was adopted in 1776. The symmetry of their deaths on the nation's 50th birthday stunned Americans and added a mythic quality to their legacies.
- Another Founder Follows: Just five years later, James Monroe, the fifth U.S. President, and another Founding Father, also died on July 4, in 1831. That's three out of the first five presidents who died on Independence Day.

To Learn More

- NCC Staff. "Three Presidents Die on July 4: Just a Coincidence?" *National Constitution Center,* July 4, 2022. This article explores the striking fact that three U.S. presidents—Adams, Jefferson, and Monroe—all died on Independence Day, raising questions about coincidence and symbolism in American history. https://tinyurl.com/july4th-death-coincidence
- Resyndicated. "Deaths of John Adams, Thomas Jefferson and James Monroe - On the 4th of July." *YouTube,* November 30, 2022. This video revisits the

historic and eerie timing of three presidential deaths on July 4, linking national destiny with personal fate. https://tinyurl.com/July4th-coincidence-video
- Webster, Daniel. "Eulogy for Adams and Jefferson." *Great Hearts Institute.* In this moving eulogy, Daniel Webster honors the legacies of Adams and Jefferson, reflecting on their shared role in American independence and their remarkable deaths on the anniversary of that independence. https://tinyurl.com/eulogy-for-adams-and-jefferson

A DAM STRANGE COINCIDENCE: THE TIERNEYS AND THE HOOVER DAM

The Hoover Dam is one of America's most incredible engineering triumphs. It is a concrete colossus straddling the Colorado River, taming floods, generating power, and holding back an inland sea. But buried within its immense structure lies a human story so eerie, so perfectly tragic, you'd swear it was scripted by fate.

Our tale begins on December 20, 1922, years before the first drop of concrete was poured. A surveyor named J.G. Tierney was working along the Colorado River, scouting locations for what would become the Hoover Dam. It was a rugged country, full of risk. As a storm rolled in, Tierney was caught in a flash flood and drowned. He became, by many accounts, the first person to die in connection with what would become the Hoover Dam project.

Jump to December 20, 1935. The dam was nearly complete. Towering above the river, the dam required backbreaking labor, daring heights, and innovations that pushed the limits of the 1930s. On that very day, tragedy struck again. A worker fell from the scaffolding to his death. His name? Patrick Tierney, J.G. Tierney's son.

The first man to die in connection with the Hoover Dam and the last man to die during its construction were father and son. And both deaths occurred on December 20.

Same place. Same day. Same family. First and last to die connected to the Hoover Dam.

Over 100 people lost their lives during the dam's construction. But only two deaths are tied together by name, date, and bloodline: a father and a son whose stories are beneath 6.6 million tons of concrete.

Was it destiny? A grim quirk of fate? Or is it just a statistical fluke made all the more haunting by the symbolism of a structure built to defy nature? Whatever you believe, the story of the Tierneys gives an eerie human note to one of America's proudest engineering feats.

Fascinating Facts

- First and Last: J.G. Tierney was the *first* to die in connection with the dam. His son Patrick was the *last* to die during its construction—13 years to the day after his father.

- Date with Destiny: Both deaths occurred on December 20, a date now known to Hoover Dam historians as one of the strangest coincidences in engineering history.
- Dam Numbers: Over 100 workers died during the dam's construction, but this father-son pairing is the only recorded case with such a dramatic familial echo.

To Learn More

- Brean, Henry. "Father and son died on the same day, 14 years apart, while working on Hoover Dam." *Las Vegas Review-Journal*, December 18, 2016. This article tells the astonishing and tragic story of Patrick and Michael Tierney, a father and son who both died while working on Hoover Dam. https://tinyurl.com/father-son-hoover-dam-deaths
- "The Tierneys and the Hoover Dam." *Window Through Time*, June 25, 2018. This post reflects on the eerie coincidence of two generations of the Tierney family dying on the same date during the construction of Hoover Dam, bookending a monumental project with personal loss. https://tinyurl.com/tierneys-and-the-hoover-dam

EERIE PATTERNS BEHIND A NATIONAL TRAGEDY

The events of September 11, 2001, were among the most tragic and transformative in modern history. But in the wake of heartbreak, something curious emerged. A pattern. A string of odd coincidences involving the numbers 9 and 11 that felt too perfect, too symmetrical, too eerie.

Start with the obvious: the date 9/11. In the U.S., 911 is the emergency number. It's also shorthand now for the event itself, a date transformed into a symbol of crisis and resilience.

Now look at the Twin Towers. Before they fell, they stood tall in Manhattan like a massive number 11 etched into the skyline—identical, side-by-side, symbols of strength and symmetry.

And then there's Flight 11—the first plane to strike. That's where the numerological rabbit hole begins.

But the pattern doesn't end there. Let's take a little numerological tour:

- Flight 11 was the first to hit. It had 92 people onboard (9 + 2 = 11).
- Flight 77, which struck the Pentagon, carried 65 people (6 + 5 = 11).

BIZARRE COINCIDENCES & SYNCHRONICITIES | 175

- The total number of victims on all hijacked planes was 246 (2 + 4 + 6 = 12. *Fact check*: not 11 as often erroneously reported).
- New York City, the city where the event took place, has a total of 11 letters. New York is the 11th state of the USA.
- Afghanistan, the country where the real perpetrators of the attack hid, has a total of 11 letters.
- The tragedy occurred on the 254th day of the year (2 + 5 + 4 = 11).
- Even the letters in "New York City" add up to 11.

Coincidence? Probably. Fascinating? Absolutely.

Human brains are natural pattern-seeking machines. We connect dots, even when they're scattered across time and space. It's how we make sense of things, especially things that shake us to our core.

So, while the number 11 appears in multiple ways related to 9/11, that doesn't mean there's a hidden code or cosmic signal. More likely, it's our minds doing what they're wired to do: create order out of disorder. This is apophenia, the tendency to perceive meaningful connections in unrelated things. Understanding apophenia doesn't ruin the magic. It deepens the mystery. It reminds us of the power of the human mind and how much we crave meaning when the world turns upside down.

Fascinating Facts

- Numerical Echo: The date 9/11 adds up: 9 + 1 + 1 = 11. Coincidentally, "9-1-1" is also the U.S. emergency number.
- The Twin Towers stood like a giant number 11 on the skyline.
- The first plane that crashed into the Twin Towers had flight number 11. Flight number 11 carried 92 people (9+2 = 11). The total number of victims in the hijacked planes was 254 (2+5+4 = 11).

To Learn More

- Mikkelson, Barabara. "9/11 Coincidences." *Snopes Fact Check,* December 11, 2005. This fact-checking article investigates widely circulated 9/11 "coincidences," separating intriguing numerology from verifiable fact. https://tinyurl.com/911-coincidences-fact-check
- Poulsen, Bruce. "Being Amused by Apophenia." *Psychology Today,* July 31, 2012. This article explores apophenia—the human tendency to find patterns in random information and how it fuels beliefs in coincidences and conspiracies. https://tinyurl.com/being-amused-by-apophenia
- "September 11: Coincidences related to the number 11 that leave you speechless!" *Telegrafi*. This piece explores the eerie numerical connections associated with the number 11 and the events of September 11. https://tinyurl.com/eerie-911-coincidences

CARL JUNG'S MEANINGFUL COINCIDENCES

Is there a larger idea that ties all these coincidences together? You've probably had one of those moments: you think of an old friend you haven't talked to in years, and then they call. Or you're deep in thought about a problem when the perfect answer pops up on a passing billboard. Most people call that a coincidence. Carl Jung called it *synchronicity*, and he didn't think it was random at all.

Jung wasn't your average lab coat type. He studied Freud, yes, but he also explored alchemy, mythology, dreams, Eastern philosophy, and even astrology. If the human mind was a house, Jung didn't just tour the living room. He opened every hidden door, climbed into the attic, and investigated the basement with a lantern and a notebook. And it was during this intellectual exploration that he stumbled on the idea of synchronicity.

Jung described synchronicity as "a meaningful coincidence." It is when two or more events are connected not by cause and effect but by *meaning*. In his view, when something out in the world lines up perfectly with something inside your psyche, you've stumbled into a moment of synchronicity. It's when the odds seem too wild. But more than that, the moment feels *personal*.

One of Jung's most famous examples happened during a therapy session. His patient, a very rational woman, was recounting a dream about a golden scarab beetle. At that exact moment, a real beetle (a scarabaeid, no less) tapped at the window. Jung opened it and handed the insect to her. She was startled and suddenly emotionally unlocked. Coincidence? Maybe. But to Jung, the timing, the symbol, and the psychological breakthrough were too perfect not to matter. They intersected in a meaningful way, an internal moment mirrored by an external event. That, to him, was synchronicity.

Jung even teamed up with physicist Wolfgang Pauli (of quantum physics fame) to explore the possibility that synchronicity had scientific footing. The two danced around ideas like time, causality, and even how the unconscious mind might interact with the fabric of reality. Jung didn't claim to *prove* anything, only that sometimes the universe seemed to sync up with the psyche in deeply personal and symbolic ways.

Critics, of course, rolled their eyes. Statisticians muttered about probabilities. But Jung didn't care. He wasn't offering a theory of everything, just an invitation to look closer when life feels uncanny. Synchronicity wasn't about fortune-telling or fate. It was about recognizing those strange intersections between the outer world and your inner world. He believed you should treat them as clues, not noise.

What's especially fascinating is that you don't have to believe in magic to appreciate synchronicity. Whether it's a glitch in the Matrix, a trick of the subconscious, or the universe showing off, these moments crack open our sense of reality and make space for mystery. You walk away with that feeling: *something about that moment mattered.*

So, when coincidence strikes, when the timing feels too perfect, when life lines up like a secret message, pause. Don't rush to explain it away. Let it sit. Let it echo.

Because maybe, just maybe, something inside you and something outside you shook hands for a brief, extraordinary second.

Fascinating Facts

- The Scarab Incident: One of Jung's most famous examples of synchronicity involved a patient recounting a dream about a golden scarab beetle, just as a real scarab beetle tapped at the window during their session. This moment marked a psychological breakthrough and helped define his theory of meaningful coincidence.
- Science Meets Soul: Jung collaborated with Nobel Prize-winning physicist Wolfgang Pauli to explore the possible relationship between synchronicity and quantum theory. Their collaboration was an early attempt to bridge the gap between psychology and physics, exploring the mysterious connections between the psyche and matter.
- Coined in 1952: The term "synchronicity" officially entered the psychological lexicon with Jung's 1952 essay *"Synchronicity: An Acausal Connecting Principle,"* published alongside a case study on astrology. Jung introduced the term as a way to describe meaningful events that defy conventional logic and causality.

To Learn More

- Broks, Paul. "Are Coincidences Real?" *The Guardian*, April 13, 2023. This article examines the psychology and science behind coincidences, questioning whether they're merely statistical flukes or something more profound. https://tinyurl.com/are-coincidences-real
- True Meaning. "Synchronicity - Why Meaningful Patterns Are Not Coincidences." *YouTube*, November 11, 2023. This video explains how meaningful coincidences—known as synchronicities—might reveal deeper patterns in life that defy logical explanations. https://tinyurl.com/synchronicity-video
- The Living Philosophy. "Carl Jung's Synchronicity: Meaningful Patterns in Life." *YouTube*, November 17, 2024. This longer video examines Carl Jung's concept of synchronicity. https://tinyurl.com/jung-meaningful-patterns-video

CONCLUSION

THE ADVENTURE DOESN'T END HERE

Well, here we are at the end of our fact-filled expedition. But before you close this book and rejoin the "normal" world of grocery lists and email pings, let's savor the moment.

Together, we've roamed singing dunes and marveled at jellyfish that laugh in the face of death. We've peeked behind history's curtain to witness dancing plagues, presidential peculiarities, and emu uprisings. We've explored the unassuming glory of everyday things. How your toothbrush traces back to jail-time ingenuity or how a snack born of spite became the potato chip we can't stop eating.

And just when you thought we'd run out of oddities, we ventured into the tangled web of cosmic coincidences, pattern-loving brains, and the eerie concept of synchronicity. It turns out that reality is weirder and far more wonderful than we ever imagined.

But here's the best part. Every single chapter, every story, every eyebrow-raising fact we explored has all been in the service of one simple mission: to celebrate your curiosity. This book wasn't written for experts, academics, or know-it-alls. It was written for the endlessly inquisitive soul who still asks, "*Wait, is that true?*" and then dives in to find out.

You see, I believe curiosity isn't just a personality trait. It's a superpower. In a world that often wants you to scroll, skim, and move on, curiosity urges you to pause, wonder, and dig deeper. It reminds you that no matter your age, background, or beliefs, there is always something new to learn, to marvel at, and to share.

So, where do we go from here? *Anywhere you like.*

Let this book be your springboard. Chase the topics that made your brain do somersaults. Start a conversation with that friend who always has the best *"Did you know..."* stories. Better yet, become that friend.

And before I go, allow me this final thank-you. Thank you for taking the time to read this book, for giving it your attention, and for bringing your wonderfully curious mind to it. I hope these pages have brought you delight, surprise, and a whole new appreciation for just how strange and magical our world really is.

To paraphrase Albert Einstein, *"The important thing is not to stop questioning. Curiosity has its own reason for existing."* And I couldn't agree more.

Make a Difference with Your Review
Your Words Help Spark Curiosity in Others

Did you enjoy discovering the strange, the fascinating, and the utterly mind-blowing truths in this book? Then you can help others experience that same sense of wonder.

Many readers decide what to pick up next based on reviews. A few honest words from you can go a long way toward helping someone else—maybe a lifelong learner, a trivia buff, or a curious teen—find this book and fall in love with learning all over again.

To share your thoughts, simply scan the QR code below:

Thank you so much for being a part of this curiosity-loving community!

Warmly,

- Gloria Lembo

REFERENCES

CHAPTER 1

3D Sailor. "Humpback whales sing beautifully." *YouTube*, August 31, 2022. https://www.youtube.com/watch?v=V9IJZsp4yyc

American Museum of Natural History. "The Talented Mimic Octopus." *American Museum of Natural History*. https://www.amnh.org/explore/news-blogs/mimic-octopus-behavior

Briggs, Helen and Gill, Victoria. "Whale song mystery solved by scientists." *BBC News*, February 21, 2024. https://www.bbc.com/news/science-environment-68358414

Campbell, Heather. "Ants: A Visual Guide." *Princeton University Press*, 2023

CBS & San Diego. "Why one young elephant's behavior stood out during earthquake felt at San Diego Zoo." *YouTube*, April 15, 2025. https://www.youtube.com/watch?v=I-j53W96X6o

Ebs, Dylan. "25 Facts About Ants." *Oh My Facts*, October 25, 2024. https://ohmyfacts.com/animals/25-facts-about-ants/

Fagaly, Steve. "Do Dolphins Really Sleep with One Eye Open?." *Dolphins and You*, May 22, 2025. https://dolphinsandyou.com/dolphins-sleep-with-one-eye-open/

Flam, Chama. "Giraffes Need Protections of Endangered Species Act After Declining Numbers, U.S. Wildlife Officials Say." *People*, November 21, 2024. https://people.com/giraffes-need-protections-of-endangered-species-u-s-wildlife-officials-say-8749177

Getty Images TV. "Mimic Octopus: Master of Disguise." *YouTube*, October 11, 2017. https://www.youtube.com/watch?v=Wos8kouz8IO

Giraffe Conservation Foundation (GCF). "Wonders of the giraffe's world." *Giraffe Conservation Foundation*. https://giraffeconservation.org/facts-about-giraffe/

Incorvaia, Darren. "Dolphins and Whales Apparently Sleep with One Eye Open." *Discover Magazine*, October 5, 2022. https://www.discovermagazine.com/planet-earth/dolphins-and-whales-apparently-sleep-with-one-eye-open

Kennerson, Elliott. "How Elephants Listen ... With Their Feet." *KQED, Deep Look*, July 17, 2018. https://www.kqed.org/science/1926248/how-elephants-listen-with-their-feet

Live Science. "Dolphins Keep an Eye Out While Sleeping." *Live Science.* https://www.livescience.com/7763-dolphins-eye-sleeping.html

Marchand, Anna. "Unraveling Mysteries of Humpback Whale Song." *NOAA National Marine Sanctuaries*, September, 2022. https://sanctuaries.noaa.gov/news/sep22/mysteries-of-humpback-whale-song.html

Masson, Jeffrey Moussaieff and McCarthy, Susan. "When Elephants Weep: The Emotional Lives of Animals." *Random House Publishing Group*, 1996

McManamna, Spencer. "Ant Colony Structure and Hierarchy." *Insect Lore*, August 08, 2024. https://www.insectlore.com/blogs/ants/ant-colony-structure-and-hierarchy?srsltid=AfmBOopf2jnUuKcBaJ95R5Ix9QOzl7yNCge1XlhuI2P-WkbtcIgxVQaa

NYU Tandon School of Engineering. "New research explores how ant colonies regulate group behaviors." *NYU Tandon*, July 11, 2024. https://engineering.nyu.edu/news/new-research-explores-how-ant-colonies-regulate-group-behaviors

Nat Geo Animals. "Mantis Shrimp Packs a Punch, Predator in Paradise." *YouTube*, May 29, 2019. https://www.youtube.com/watch?v=E0Li1k5hGBE

Nightingale, Sarah. "Mantis shrimp inspires next generation of ultra-strong materials." *University of California*, May 31, 2016. https://www.universityofcalifornia.edu/news/mantis-shrimp-inspires-next-generation-ultra-strong-materials

Osterloff, Emily. "Immortal jellyfish: the secret to cheating death." *Natural History Museum.* https://www.nhm.ac.uk/discover/immortal-jellyfish-secret-to-cheating-death.html

Orozco, Trizzy. *"Why the Immortal Jellyfish May Never Die and What That Means for Aging."* Discover Wild Science, May 6, 2025. https://discoverwildscience.com/why-the-immortal-jellyfish-may-never-die-and-what-that-means-for-aging-1-305448/

Parker, Laura. "Rare Video Shows Elephants 'Mourning' Matriarch's Death." *National Geographic*, August 21, 2016. https://www.nationalgeographic.com/animals/article/elephants-mourning-video-animal-grief

Pinoy Insight TV. "The Exploding Ants That Die Like Tiny Warriors." *YouTube.* https://www.youtube.com/watch?v=DjQIcMJdv1o

Real Science. "The Incredible Way This Jellyfish Goes Back in Time." *YouTube*, May 21, 2022. https://www.youtube.com/watch?v=DSLQYTt8BjA

Robinson, Lizzie. "30 Most Random Facts About Giraffes." *The Fact Site*, April 1, 2025. https://www.thefactsite.com/random-giraffe-facts/

Sammann, Stephanie. "How Pigeons Always Find Their Way Home." *Real Science YouTube*, June 12, 2022. https://www.youtube.com/watch?app=desktop&v=4DkMVCzvgRg

Sammann, Stephanie. "The Insane Biology of Ant Colonies." *Real Science YouTube*, February 6, 2021. https://www.youtube.com/watch?v=VLBDVXLiWxQ

Spencer, Erin. "Why the Mimic Octopus is the Ultimate Master of Disguise." *Ocean Conservancy Blog*, April 2022. https://oceanconservancy.org/blog/2016/04/01/why-the-mimic-octopus-is-the-ultimate-master-of-disguise/

Stuff to Blow Your Mind. "5 Amazing Giraffe Facts – Science on the Web #51." *YouTube*, April 20, 2014. https://www.youtube.com/watch?v=OxTh7cXRPrI

Tsavo Trust. "How tall is a giraffe (and other giraffe facts)." *Tsavo Trust*. https://tsavotrust.org/how-tall-is-a-giraffe-and-other-giraffe-facts/

Weber, Chris. "Did You Know a Certain Jellyfish Can Live Forever? Here's the Science!" *Animals Around the Globe*, May 3, 2025. https://www.animalsaroundtheglobe.com/did-you-know-a-certain-jellyfish-can-live-forever-heres-the-science-2-298241/

Whale and Dolphin Conservation (WDC). "How do dolphins sleep?." *WDC*. https://us.whales.org/whales-dolphins/how-do-dolphins-sleep

Wikipedia. "Colobopsis saundersi." *Wikipedia*. https://en.wikipedia.org/wiki/Colobopsis_saundersi

Wikipedia. "Elephant cognition." *Wikipedia*. https://en.wikipedia.org/wiki/Elephant_cognition

Wikipedia. "Mimic octopus." *Wikipedia*. https://en.wikipedia.org/wiki/Mimic_octopus

Xiang, Annie. "How Pigeons Find Their Home? The Secrets Behind Their Incredible Homing Ability." *Birdfly Blog*, September 18, 2024. https://www.birdfy.com/blogs/blogs/how-pigeons-find-their-home-the-secrets-behind-their-incredible-homing-ability?sscid=61k9_jvwmr&

CHAPTER 2

American Museum of Natural History. "Do Trees Talk to Each Other?." *Ask Smithsonian*, March 2018. https://www.smithsonianmag.com/science-nature/the-whispering-trees-180968084/

Ash, Arvin. "Quantum Entanglement Explained - How does it really work?." *YouTube*, July 30, 2021. https://www.youtube.com/watch?v=unb_yoj1Usk

Ashford, Brittany. "Bioluminescent Bays Puerto Rico." *Puerto Rico.com*, 2025. https://www.puertorico.com/bioluminescent-bays

Attenborough, David. "David Attenborough Encounters a Symbiotic Fungi!." *YouTube Nature Bites*, February 7, 2022. https://www.youtube.com/watch?v=kbIDpHNq_fA

BBC. "These fungi facts will blow your mind." *YouTube*, February 18, 2022. https://www.youtube.com/watch?v=_Dyuj-RI3Jk

Borneman, Elizabeth. "Ice Circles." *Geography Realm*, February 27, 2019. https://www.geographyrealm.com/ice-circles/

Caltech Science Exchange. "What Is Entanglement and Why Is It Important?." *Caltech Science Exchange*. https://scienceexchange.caltech.edu/topics/quantum-science-explained/entanglement

Cole, Brendan. "Physicists Have Finally Figured Out Why These Massive Ice Discs Start Spinning on Their Own." *Science Alert*, March 30, 2016. https://www.sciencealert.com/physicists-have-finally-figured-out-why-these-massive-ice-discs-suddenly-start-spinning

Cox, Brian. "Brian Cox Explains the Fermi Paradox." *Science Time, YouTube*, March 8, 2025. https://www.youtube.com/watch?v=NbNPBcUgDTs

Davies, Paul. "The Eerie Silence: Renewing Our Search for Alien Intelligence." *Houghton Mifflin Harcourt*, 2010

D'Iorio, Jen. "How Much Does a Cloud Weigh?." *Weather Works*, March 19, 2021. https://weatherworksinc.com/news/how-much-does-a-cloud-weigh

EarthDate. "Singing Sand Dunes." *EarthDate*, September 12, 2023. https://www.earthdate.org/episodes/singing-sand-dunes

Fischer, Shannon. "Singing Sand Dunes Explained." *National Geographic*, October 21, 2012. https://www.nationalgeographic.com/science/article/121031-singing-sand-dunes-physics-science-whistling

Graham, Adam H. "Japan's mysterious glowing squid." *BBC Travel*, February 24, 2022. https://www.bbc.com/travel/article/20150505-japans-mysterious-glowing-squid

REFERENCES | 189

Grant, Richard. "Do Trees Talk to Each Other?." *Ask Smithsonian*, March 2018. https://www.smithsonianmag.com/science-nature/the-whispering-trees-180968084/

Hofeldt, Alex. "How small are we in the scale of the universe?." *TED-Ed*, *YouTube*, February 13, 2017. https://www.youtube.com/watch?v=WYQ3O8U6SMY

Matt Miller Film. "Bio Bays in Puerto Rico – Everything you need to know!." *Vos Travel with Kids*, *YouTube*, January 24, 2025. https://www.youtube.com/watch?v=kvhvOZrKMUs

Nalewicki, Jennifer. "Puerto Rico's Bioluminescent Bays Are Brighter Than Ever." *Smithsonian Magazine*, April 6, 2022. https://www.smithsonianmag.com/travel/puerto-ricos-bioluminescent-bays-are-brighter-than-ever-180979874/

NASA. "Explore breathtaking images of distant galaxies." *Hubble Site*. https://science.nasa.gov/mission/hubble/

National Geographic. "Hidden world of microscopic life revealed in extraordinary pictures." *National Geographic*. https://www.nationalgeographic.com/science/article/hidden-world-microscopic-life-revealed-extraordinary-pictures

One Minute Explore. "Uncovering the Mystery of Singing Sand Dunes." *YouTube*, April 16, 2023. https://youtu.be/VDqSBb8QuAY?si=WlnqXUInLkn-xuKj

Pappas, Stephanie. "Do Trees Really Support Each Other through a Network of Fungi?." *Scientific American*, February 13, 2023. https://www.scientificamerican.com/article/do-trees-support-each-other-through-a-network-of-fungi/

Rober, Mark. "How Much Do Clouds Actually Weigh?." *YouTube*, February 17, 2016. https://www.youtube.com/watch?v=hREKZIyIbvg

Schlickenmeyer, Max. "The Most Astounding Fact – Neil deGrasse Tyson." *YouTube*, March 2, 2012. https://youtube.com/watch?v=9D05ej8u-gU

Science Channel. "This is How Nature Produces Perfect Ice Discs." *YouTube*, December 30, 2016. https://www.youtube.com/watch?v=zsAQoxJdnMI&t=5s

Science Section, Library of Congress. "How Much Does a Cloud Weigh?." *Library of Congress*, October 27, 2023. https://www.loc.gov/everyday-mysteries/meteorology-climatology/item/how-much-does-a-cloud-weigh/

SETI Institute. https://www.seti.org

Sheldrake, Merlin. "Entangled Life: How Fungi Make Our Worlds, Change Our Minds & Shape Our Futures." *Random House*, May 12, 2020

Siegel, Ethan. "How Big Is the Universe's Largest Galaxy, Really?." *Big Think*, May 31, 2021. https://bigthink.com/starts-with-a-bang/how-big-is-the-universes-largest-galaxy-really/

Simard, Suzanne. "Finding the Mother Tree: Discovering the Wisdom of the Forest." *Knopf*, May 4, 2021

Simard, Suzanne. "How Trees Talk to Each Other." *TED Talk*, June 2016. https://www.ted.com/talks/suzanne_simard_how_trees_talk_to_each_other

Toomey, Diane. "Exploring How and Why Trees 'Talk' to Each Other." *Yale Environment 360*, September 1, 2016. https://e360.yale.edu/features/exploring_how_and_why_trees_talk_to_each_other

U.S. Department of Energy. "Behind the Scenes: How Fungi Make Nutrients Available to the World." *Office of Science Blog*, January 31, 2018. https://www.energy.gov/science/articles/behind-scenes-how-fungi-make-nutrients-available-world

United Nations Decade on Restoration. "Benefits of Fungi for the Environment and Humans." *United Nations*. https://www.decadeonrestoration.org/stories/benefits-fungi-environment-and-humans

USGS Water Science School. "How Much Does a Cloud Weigh?." *USGS*, July 7, 2019. https://www.usgs.gov/special-topics/water-science-school/science/how-much-does-a-cloud-weigh

Watzke, Megan and Arcand, Kimberly. "Magnitude: The Scale of the Universe." *Black Dog & Leventhal*, 2017

Wikipedia. "Ice circle." *Wikipedia*. https://en.wikipedia.org/wiki/Ice_disc

Wikipedia. "Quantum Entanglement." *Wikipedia*. https://en.wikipedia.org/wiki/Quantum_entanglement

Wikipedia. "The Fermi Paradox." *Wikipedia*. https://en.wikipedia.org/wiki/Fermi_paradox

Williams, Barrett. "The Singing Sands: Unveiling the Phenomenon of Booming Dunes." Audible Audiobook, April 21, 2024

CHAPTER 3

Amelia Earhart. "." *National Air and Space Museum, Smithsonian*. https://airandspace.si.edu/explore/stories/amelia-earhart

Austin, Daryl. "Hysterical strength? Fight or Flight? This is how your body reacts to extreme stress." *National Geographic, Science*, March 19, 2024.

https://www.nationalgeographic.com/science/article/extreme-strength-fight-flight-stress-muscle-power

BBC Earth Science. "Finding the Super Tasters." YouTube, July 26, 2019. https://www.youtube.com/watch?v=aroNLSRzeno&t=11s

Be Smart. "The Weird Reason Some People Can Taste Colors." YouTube, December 30, 2024. https://www.youtube.com/watch?v=pPIem63bC4w

Biographics. "Marco Polo: The World's Greatest Explorer." YouTube, January 31, 2019. https://www.youtube.com/shorts/YOzDQItQERs

Borunda, Alejandra. "The ongoing mystery of hiccups." National Geographic Science, April 5, 2023. https://www.nationalgeographic.com/science/article/hiccups-why-how-to-get-rid-of-them-fish-ancestors

BuzzFeed Multiplayer. "How Strong Can an Adrenaline Rush Make You?." YouTube, January 1, 2018. https://youtu.be/ra-9ioNWCdU

Cheriyedath, Susha. "What is a Phantom Limb." News Medical Life & Sciences, May 6, 2021. https://www.news-medical.net/health/What-is-a-Phantom-Limb.aspx

Cleveland Clinic. "Phantom Limb Pain." Cleveland Clinic, March 7, 2024. https://my.clevelandclinic.org/health/diseases/12092-phantom-limb-pain

Cleveland Clinic. "Sleep Paralysis." Cleveland Clinic Health Library, July 3, 2024. https://my.clevelandclinic.org/health/diseases/21974-sleep-paralysis

Cleveland Clinic. "Synesthesia." Cleveland Clinic, May 3, 2023. https://my.clevelandclinic.org/health/symptoms/24995-synesthesia

Crosby, Guy. "Super-Tasters and Non-Tasters: Is it Better to Be Average?." Harvard, The Nutrition Source, May 31, 2016. https://nutritionsource.hsph.harvard.edu/2016/05/31/super-tasters-non-tasters-is-it-better-to-be-average/

Cytowic, R. E., & Eagleman, D. M.. "Wednesday is Indigo Blue: Discovering the Brain of Synesthesia." MIT Press, September 30, 2011

Daily Brain Bites. "Why Do We Hiccup? The Fascinating Science Explained!." YouTube, February 4, 2025. https://www.youtube.com/watch?v=XOGpYWAKZPA&t=5s

Encyclopedia.com. "The Journeys of Marco Polo and Their Impact." Encyclopedia.com. https://www.encyclopedia.com/science/encyclopedias-almanacs-transcripts-and-maps/journeys-marco-polo-and-their-impact

Frances, Gatta. "Why Do We Yawn?." WebMD, March 15, 2024. https://www.webmd.com/sleep-disorders/what-to-know-about-yawning

Health Essentials. "Supertasters: What It Means and How To Tell If You Are One." *Cleveland Clinic*, March 20, 2025. https://health.clevelandclinic.org/what-it-means-to-be-a-supertaster

Holland, Kimberly. "Are You a Supertaster?." *Healthline*, February 21, 2019. https://www.healthline.com/health/food-nutrition/supertaster

Jividen, Sarah. "Does the Liver Regenerate (and When Doesn't It)?." *Very Well Health*, January 6, 2025. https://www.verywellhealth.com/does-the-liver-regenerate-8722587

King, Lori. "What to Know about an Adrenaline Rush." *WebMD*, October 23, 2024. https://www.webmd.com/a-to-z-guides/what-to-know-adrenaline-rush

Know It. "10 Marvelous Facts About Liver Regeneration." *YouTube*, March 18, 2025. https://www.youtube.com/shorts/30zdF7ja8Do

NASA History. "July 20 1969: One Giant Leap for Mankind." *NASA*, July 20, 2019. https://www.nasa.gov/mission_pages/apollo/apollo11.html

Nat Geo Live. "Free Soloing with Alex Honnold." *National Geographic*, August 29, 2011. https://www.youtube.com/watch?v=leCAy1v1fnI

NPR's Skunk Bear. "Why Do We Get Goose Bumps?." *YouTube*, October 30, 2015. https://www.youtube.com/watch?v=_U5CHuJNrVI

PBS. "Marco Polo". *PBS Learning Media*. https://florida.pbslearningmedia.org/resource/ff32837d-b085-40d4-8d60-ac9a676cb857/marco-polo-pbs-world-explorers/

Plethrons. "Phantom Limbs Explained." *YouTube*, March 23, 2015. https://youtu.be/ySIDMU2cy0Y

Popiashvili, Giorgi. "Prisoners of sleep: Face to face with sleep paralysis." *Independently Published*, February 13, 2025

Reynolds, Sharon. "What goosebumps are for." *NIH, National Institutes of Health*, July 28, 2020. https://www.nih.gov/news-events/nih-research-matters/what-goosebumps-are#:

Shestopalova, Alex. "What Is Synesthesia in Music?." *KTDJ Explains - Music*, September 30, 2024. https://killthedj.com/what-is-synesthesia-in-music/

Sleep Is The Foundation. "Sleep Paralysis: What You Need To Know!." *YouTube*, November 1, 2022. https://www.youtube.com/watch?v=mQBfVpKiW64

Suni, Eric. "Sleep Paralysis." *Sleep Foundation*, June 5, 2025. https://www.sleepfoundation.org/parasomnias/sleep-paralysis

Today NBC News. "Meet Erik Weihenmayer: The Blind Adventurer Who Conquered Mount Everest and Grand Canyon." *YouTube*, July 24, 2017. https://www.youtube.com/watch?v=2Y9Jy0WzrOg

Uproxx Life Human Limits. "Dean Karnazes: The Ultramarathon Man." *YouTube*, September 18, 2017. https://www.youtube.com/watch?v=Mtp65SWoyWc

Uproxx Life Human Limits. "Wim Hof, The Iceman Cometh." *YouTube*, September 26, 2016. https://www.youtube.com/watch?v=q6XKcsm3dKs

Wikipedia. "Alex Honnold." *Wikipedia*. https://en.wikipedia.org/wiki/Alex_Honnold#Books

Wikipedia. "Dean Karnazes." *Wikipedia*. https://en.wikipedia.org/wiki/Dean_Karnazes

Wikipedia. "Liver regeneration." *Wikipedia*. https://en.wikipedia.org/wiki/Liver_regeneration

Wikipedia. "Wim Hof." *Wikipedia*. https://en.wikipedia.org/wiki/Wim_Hof

CHAPTER 4

ABC Australia. "The Great Emu War: how it started and who won." *YouTube*, December 29, 2022. https://www.youtube.com/watch?v=ejiYxSWrkdY

Amazon Studios. "The Lost City of Z – David Grann Featurette." *Prime Movies*, April 15, 2017. https://www.youtube.com/watch?v=kdu7h1mvtGI

Andrews, Evan. "The Man Who Survived Two Atomic Bombs." *History.com*. https://www.history.com/articles/the-man-who-survived-two-atomic-bombs

Andrews, Evan. "What Was the Dancing Plague of 1518?." *History.com*, August 31, 2015. https://www.history.com/articles/what-was-the-dancing-plague-of-1518

Dave Roos. "Why the Voynich Manuscript May Be the World's Most Mysterious Book." *History.com*, May 27, 2025. https://www.history.com/articles/voynich-manuscript-mystery

Epic History Facts Team. "The Time London Had a Beer Flood That Killed People." *EpicHistoryFacts.com*, March 8, 2025. https://epichistoryfacts.com/london-had-a-beer-flood-that-killed-people/

Escher, Kat. "This 1814 Beer Flood Killed Eight People." *Smithsonian Magazine*, August 4, 2017. https://www.smithsonianmag.com/smart-news/1814-beer-flood-killed-eight-people-180964256/

Forgotten History. "Dead Pope on Trial: The Cadaver Synod." *YouTube*, May 28, 2025. https://www.youtube.com/watch?v=9IQ5qpwflvo

Grann, David. "The Lost City of Z: A Tale of Deadly Obsession in the Amazon." *Vintage*, February 17, 2009

Handwerk, Brian. "Lost Cities of the Amazon Discovered From the Air." *Smithsonian Magazine*, May 25, 2022. https://www.smithsonianmag.com/science-nature/lost-cities-of-the-amazon-discovered-from-the-air-180980142/

Harper, Elizabeth. "The Cadaver Synod: When a Pope's Corpse Was Put on Trial." *Atlas Obscura*, March 3, 2014. https://www.atlasobscura.com/articles/morbid-monday-cadaver-synod

History. "Amazing Survivor Lives Through Two Nuclear Explosions." *YouTube*, August 21, 2022. https://www.youtube.com/watch?v=c0-YxYM0Gi8

History.com Staff. "What Happened to the 'Lost Colony' of Roanoke? How could 115 people just vanish?." *History.com*, October 03, 2012. https://www.history.com/articles/what-happened-to-the-lost-colony-of-roanoke

History Skills. "The Cadaver Synod: when the Catholic Church dug up a dead pope to put his corpse on trial." *History Skills*. https://www.historyskills.com/classroom/ancient-history/cadaver-synod

History Thumbprint. "The Beer Flood of 1814." *YouTube*, March 13, 2024. https://www.youtube.com/watch?v=iN20O3UjlR8

Incredible Stories. "The Lost Colony of Roanoke: One of America's Greatest Mysteries." *YouTube*, May 5, 2025. https://www.youtube.com/watch?v=pu_9ntet6H4&t=811s

Klingaman, William K. and Klingaman, Nicholas. "The Year Without Summer: 1816 and the Volcano That Darkened the World and Changed History." *St. Martin's Griffin*, March 11, 2014

Landrigan, Dan and Landrigan, Leslie. "1816: The Year Without a Summer." *New England Historical Society*. https://newenglandhistoricalsociety.com/1816-year-without-a-summer/

Lawler, Andrew. "The Secret Token: Myth, Obsession, and the Search for the Lost Colony of Roanoke." *Anchor*, June 4, 2019

Nick's Not Niche. "They DANCED till they DIED: The Dancing Plague of 1518." *YouTube*, May 30, 2023. https://www.youtube.com/watch?v=s0j3BkQMB54

OzGeology. "The Notorious 1815 Eruption of Mount Tambora." *YouTube*, November 1, 2023. https://www.youtube.com/watch?v=leSBmWoEMp4

Pellegrino, Charles. "To Hell and Back: The Last Train from Hiroshima." *Rowman & Littlefield Publishers*, February 7, 2019

Rosalind Jana. "The people who 'danced themselves to death'." *BBC*, May 12, 2022. https://www.bbc.com/culture/article/20220512-the-people-who-danced-themselves-to-death

Roller, Sarah. "10 Facts About Percy Fawcett and the Lost City of Z." History Hit, November 12, 2021. https://www.historyhit.com/facts-about-percy-fawcett-and-the-lost-city-of-z/

Sci NC, PBS North Carolina. "New Clues to the Fate of the Lost Colony." *YouTube*, January 20, 2017. https://www.youtube.com/watch?v=pL4hu7k4tGw&t=5s

Travers, Scott. "The Real Story Behind Australia's Great Emu 'War' Of 1932 (And Why They Lost—Twice)." *Forbes.com*, December 26, 2024. https://www.forbes.com/sites/scotttravers/2024/12/26/the-real-story-behind-australias-great-emu-war-of-1932-and-why-they-lost-twice/

Waller, John. "The Dancing Plague: The Strange, True Story of an Extraordinary Illness." *Sourcebooks*, September 1, 2009

Wikipedia. "Emu War." *Wikipedia*. https://en.wikipedia.org/wiki/Emu_War

Wikipedia. "Voynich manuscript." *Wikipedia*. https://en.wikipedia.org/wiki/Voynich_manuscript

Wikipedia. "Year Without a Summer." *Wikipedia*. https://en.wikipedia.org/wiki/Year_Without_a_Summer

Yale. "Voynich Manuscript." *Beinecke Rare Book & Manuscript Library*. https://beinecke.library.yale.edu/collections/highlights/voynich-manuscript

Yale Press. "What We Know About the Voynich Manuscript." *YouTube*, December 2, 2016. https://www.youtube.com/watch?v=kFfAICkC4Pc

CHAPTER 5

ACS Chemistry for Life. "Discovery and Development of Penicillin." *ACS.org*. https://www.acs.org/education/whatischemistry/landmarks/flemingpenicillin.html

APS Advancing Physics. "November 8, 1895: Roentgen's Discovery of X-Rays." *APS News*, November 1, 2002. https://www.aps.org/apsnews/2001/11/1895-roentgens-discovery-xrays

Avishkaar Nexus. "Who Invented the Toothbrush? A 5000-Year Tale of Clean Teeth." *YouTube*, Nov 28, 2024. https://www.youtube.com/watch?v=xeiI5mYZXIY&t=3s

Berger, Harold. "The Mystery of a New Kind of Rays: The Story of Wilhelm Conrad Roentgen and His Discovery of X-Rays." CreateSpace Independent Publishing, September 6, 2012.

Cooks Info. "Kellogg's Cereal Company Founded 19 February" *Cooksinfo.com.* https://www.cooksinfo.com/kelloggs-cereal-company-founded

Cosi's Science Now. "How Did Nature's Design Lead to Velcro's Creation? | COSI's Science Now with Dr. Marci Howdyshell." *YouTube*, March 19, 2020. https://www.youtube.com/watch?v=3jHy9v5PUpo

Daily Dose Documentary. "History of Potato Chips: Who Invented the Potato Chip?" *YouTube*, Jun 13, 2023 https://www.youtube.com/watch?v=R-JGdJh5LyM

Daugherty, Greg. "Who Invented the Potato Chip? It's Complicated." *History Channel*, February 03, 2021 https://www.history.com/articles/who-invented-potato-chip-saratoga

Girdley, Michael. "The Invention of Velcro." *YouTube*, August 27, 2024. https://www.youtube.com/shorts/-etDhmopBdU

Gross, Terry. "How The 'Battling' Kellogg Brothers Revolutionized American Breakfast." *NPR, The Salt*, August 8, 2017 https://www.npr.org/sections/thesalt/2017/08/08/542145177/how-the-battling-kellogg-brothers-revolutionized-american-breakfast

History at Home. "The Remarkable History of Toilet Paper." *YouTube*, April 27, 2020. https://www.youtube.com/watch?v=5vZ4-UHszs4

History of Food. "Kellogg's: The Breakfast Revolution!" *YouTube*, Feb 19, 2025 https://www.youtube.com/watch?v=fcC7WS0fZdo

History of ideas. "The Accidental Invention That Changed Kitchens Forever: The Microwave!" *YouTube*, Nov 5, 2024. https://www.youtube.com/watch?v=lvxVz-Zik3Y

Mediphysman. "Discovery of the Xray." *YouTube*, June 27, 2024. https://www.youtube.com/watch?v=jmQ_JYbAel8

NBC News Learn. "Chance Discoveries: Post-It Notes." *YouTube*, May 2, 2020 https://www.youtube.com/watch?v=bvalMbOdseU

PBS. "The Discovery of Penicillin." *PBS Learning Media*, December 25, 2015 https://florida.pbslearningmedia.org/resource/odys08.sci.life.gen.discovery/the-discovery-of-penicillin/

Ponti, Crystal. "All the Ways We've Wiped: The History of Toilet Paper and What Came Before." *History.com*, April 15, 2020. https://www.history.com/articles/toilet-paper-hygiene-ancient-rome-china

REFERENCES | 197

Ponti, Crystal. "Who Invented the Microwave Oven?" *History.com*, April 28, 2025. https://www.history.com/articles/microwave-oven-invention

Post-It. "History Timeline: Post-It notes." *Post-it.com*. https://www.post-it.com/3M/en_US/post-it/contact-us/about-us/

Pruitt, Sarah. "Cereal: The Accidental Invention That Changed American Breakfast." *History.com*. https://www.history.com/articles/cereal-breakfast-origins-kellogg

Sutter, Emily. "The evolution of the toothbrush." *Dental Tribune*, March 31, 2011   https://us.dental-tribune.com/news/the-evolution-of-the-toothbrush/

The History Guy. "Toothpaste: A History of Oral Hygiene." *YouTube*. May 22, 2023. https://www.youtube.com/watch?v=ODmJJSaoYv8

Velcro. "Securing Success for NASA Astronauts." *Velcro.com*. https://www.velcro.com/original-thinking/securing-success-for-nasa-astronauts/

Velcro Companies. "An Idea that Stuck: How George de Mestral Invented the Velcro Brand Fastener." *Velcro.com blog*, November 11, 2016. https://www.velcro.com/news-and-blog/2016/11/an-idea-that-stuck-how-george-de-mestral-invented-the-velcro-fastener/

Warner, Deborah. "A brush with history." *Smithsonian, National Museum of American History*, October 31, 2022. https://americanhistory.si.edu/explore/stories/brush-history

Weird History. "The History of Toilets." *YouTube*, January 12, 2020. https://www.youtube.com/watch?v=TaSrf2DNy5w

Wikipedia. "Discovery of penicillin." *Wikipedia*. https://en.wikipedia.org/wiki/Discovery_of_penicillin

Wikipedia. "Post-it note." *Wikipedia*. https://en.wikipedia.org/wiki/Post-it_note

Wikipedia. "Toilet". *Wikipedia*. https://en.wikipedia.org/wiki/Toilet#Gallery

CHAPTER 6

Brean, Henry. "Father and son died on the same day, 14 years apart while working on Hoover Dam." Las Vegas Review-Journal, December 18, 2016. https://www.reviewjournal.com/local/local-las-vegas/father-and-son-died-on-the-same-day-14-years-apart-while-working-on-hoover-dam/

Broks, Paul. "Are Coincidences Real?" *The Guardian*, April 13, 2023. https://www.theguardian.com/world/2023/apr/13/are-coincidences-real

Cambray, Joe. "Synchronicity: An Acausal Connecting Principle." *International Association for Analytical Psychology*. https://iaap.org/jung-analytical-psychology/short-articles-on-analytical-psychology/synchronicity-an-acausal-connecting-principle/

Chen, Edwin. "Twins Reared Apart: A Living Lab." *The New York Times*, December 9, 1979. https://www.nytimes.com/1979/12/09/archives/twins-reared-apart-a-living-lab.html

Dison, Brad. "The Lost Book." *Natchitoches Parish Journal*, May 11, 2022. https://natchitochesparishjournal.com/2022/05/11/the-lost-book/

Hancox, John. "Curious England: Strange Tales from England's Past." *Facebook.com*, July 13, 2024. https://www.facebook.com/groups/curiousengland/posts/1873259809808336/

HaveSomeFun 3344. "Johnny Carson Memories: The Jim Twins." *YouTube*, December 1, 2022. https://www.youtube.com/watch?v=27hI8-mZkO4

Knight, Jonathan. "The Lincoln-Kennedy Coincidences: Fact and Legend in the Assassinations." *Exposit Books*, January 6, 2023.

Leith, Sam. "What are you doing here? Or why seemingly amazing coincidences aren't so unlikely after all." *Daily Mail.com*, April 2, 2011. https://www.dailymail.co.uk/home/moslive/article-1371572/Seemingly-amazing-coincidences-unlikely-all.html

Mikkelson, Barabara. "9/11 Coincidences." *Snopes Fact Check*, December 11, 2005. https://www.snopes.com/fact-check/coincidences/

Mikkelson, David. "Are These 'Coincidences' Linking Lincoln to Kennedy Real?" *Snopes Fact Check*, June 11, 1999. https://www.snopes.com/fact-check/linkin-kennedy/

Mr. Beat. "All Those Weird Lincoln Kennedy Coincidences." *YouTube*, April 9, 2021. https://www.youtube.com/watch?v=te6yiRProhs

NCC Staff. "Three Presidents Die on July 4th: Just a Coincidence?" *National Constitution Center*, July 4, 2022. https://constitutioncenter.org/blog/three-presidents-die-on-july-4th-just-a-coincidence

"Patrick William Tierney." *Obit in Springfield Newspaper*, December 1935. https://www.findagrave.com/memorial/32888771/patrick_william-tierney

Poulsen, Bruce. "Being Amused by Apophenia." *Psychology Today*, July 31, 2012. https://www.psychologytoday.com/us/blog/reality-play/201207/being-amused-by-apophenia

Resyndicated. "Deaths of John Adams, Thomas Jefferson and James Monroe - On the 4th of July." *YouTube*, November 30, 2022. https://www.youtube.com/watch?v=9WAIY92MLU0

Shaw, Gabbi. "A novella published 14 years before the Titanic sank seemed to have predicted the disaster." *Business Insider*, June 28, 2023. https://www.businessinsider.com/novel-futility-similarities-with-titanic-2023-6

Taylor, C. James. "John Adams: Life After the Presidency." *UVA, Miller Center*. https://millercenter.org/president/adams/life-after-the-presidency

Taylor, Tom. "How Anthony Hopkins became the centre of the quantum theory of coincidence." *Far Out*, April 21, 2023. https://faroutmagazine.co.uk/how-anthony-hopkins-became-the-centre-of-the-quantum-theory-of-coincidence/

Telegrafi. "September 11: Coincidences related to the number 11, that leave you speechless!" *Telegrafi.com*. https://telegrafi.com/en/September-11%2C-coincidences-related-to-the-number-11-that-will-leave-you-speechless/

The Living Philosophy. "Carl Jung's Synchronicity: Meaningful Patterns in Life." *YouTube*, November 17, 2024. https://www.youtube.com/watch?v=jjc9KULop3c

The Tierneys and the Hoover Dam. *Window Through Time*, June 25, 2018. https://windowthroughtime.wordpress.com/tag/father-and-son-killed-14-years-apart/

Tiger Media Network. "Wreck Of The Titan: A foretelling of disaster or interesting coincidence." *YouTube*, April 19, 2024. https://www.youtube.com/watch?v=KLFD7NKlDSo

Tikkanen, Amy. "Titanic." *Encyclopedia Britannica*, June 5, 2025. https://www.britannica.com/topic/Titanic

True Meaning. "Synchronicity - Why Meaningful Patterns Are Not Coincidences." *YouTube*, November 11, 2023. https://www.youtube.com/watch?v=r3H8lP8dChE

Webster, Daniel. "Eulogy for Adams and Jefferson." *Great Hearts Institute*. https://www.whatsoproudlywehail.org/curriculum/the-american-calendar/eulogy-for-adams-and-jefferson/

Wikipedia. "Lincoln–Kennedy coincidences urban legend." *Wikipedia*. https://en.wikipedia.org/wiki/Lincoln–Kennedy_coincidences_urban_legend

www.ingramcontent.com/pod-product-compliance
Lightning Source LLC
Chambersburg PA
CBHW060947050426
42337CB00052B/1657